T0311416

MACAT

An Analysis of

Jared M. Diamond's

Collapse
How Societies Choose
to Fail or Survive

Rodolfo Maggio

ROUTLEDGE

Published by Macat International Ltd
24:13 Coda Centre, 189 Munster Road, London SW6 6AW.

Distributed exclusively by Routledge
2 Park Square, Milton Park, Abingdon, Oxon OX14 4RN
711 Third Avenue, New York, NY 10017, USA

Routledge is an imprint of the Taylor & Francis Group, an informa business

www.macat.com
info@macat.com

Cataloguing in Publication Data
A catalogue record for this book is available from the British Library.
Library of Congress Cataloguing-in-Publication Data is available upon request.
Cover illustration: Kim Thompson

ISBN 978-1-912302-03-1 (hardback)
ISBN 978-1-912128-68-6 (paperback)
ISBN 978-1-912128-28-0 (e-book)

Notice
The information in this book is designed to orientate readers of the work under analysis,
to elucidate and contextualise its key ideas and themes, and to aid in the development
of critical thinking skills. It is not meant to be used, nor should it be used, as a
substitute for original thinking or in place of original writing or research. References and
notes are provided for informational purposes and their presence does not constitute
endorsement of the information or opinions therein. This book is presented solely for
educational purposes. It is sold on the understanding that the publisher is not engaged
to provide any scholarly advice. The publisher has made every effort to ensure that
this book is accurate and up-to-date, but makes no warranties or representations with
regard to the completeness or reliability of the information it contains. The information
and the opinions provided herein are not guaranteed or warranted to produce particular
results and may not be suitable for students of every ability. The publisher shall not be
liable for any loss, damage or disruption arising from any errors or omissions, or from
the use of this book, including, but not limited to, special, incidental, consequential or
other damages caused, or alleged to have been caused, directly or indirectly, by the
information contained within.

CONTENTS

WAYS IN TO THE TEXT

Who Is Jared M. Diamond? 9

What Does *Collapse* Say? 10

Why Does *Collapse* Matter? 12

SECTION 1: INFLUENCES

Module 1: The Author and the Historical Context 16

Module 2: Academic Context 21

Module 3: The Problem 27

Module 4: The Author's Contribution 32

SECTION 2: IDEAS

Module 5: Main Ideas 38

Module 6: Secondary Ideas 43

Module 7: Achievement 48

Module 8: Place in the Author's Work 53

SECTION 3: IMPACT

Module 9: The First Responses 58

Module 10: The Evolving Debate 64

Module 11: Impact and Influence Today 69

Module 12: Where Next? 74

Glossary of Terms 80

People Mentioned in the Text 89

Works Cited 96

THE MACAT LIBRARY

The Macat Library is a series of unique academic explorations of seminal works in the humanities and social sciences – books and papers that have had a significant and widely recognised impact on their disciplines. It has been created to serve as much more than just a summary of what lies between the covers of a great book. It illuminates and explores the influences on, ideas of, and impact of that book. Our goal is to offer a learning resource that encourages critical thinking and fosters a better, deeper understanding of important ideas.

Each publication is divided into three Sections: Influences, Ideas, and Impact. Each Section has four Modules. These explore every important facet of the work, and the responses to it.

This Section-Module structure makes a Macat Library book easy to use, but it has another important feature. Because each Macat book is written to the same format, it is possible (and encouraged!) to cross-reference multiple Macat books along the same lines of inquiry or research. This allows the reader to open up interesting interdisciplinary pathways.

To further aid your reading, lists of glossary terms and people mentioned are included at the end of this book (these are indicated by an asterisk [*] throughout) – as well as a list of works cited.

Macat has worked with the University of Cambridge to identify the elements of critical thinking and understand the ways in which six different skills combine to enable effective thinking.
Three allow us to fully understand a problem; three more give us the tools to solve it. Together, these six skills make up the **PACIER** model of critical thinking. They are:

ANALYSIS – understanding how an argument is built
EVALUATION – exploring the strengths and weaknesses of an argument
INTERPRETATION – understanding issues of meaning

CREATIVE THINKING – coming up with new ideas and fresh connections
PROBLEM-SOLVING – producing strong solutions
REASONING – creating strong arguments

To find out more, visit **WWW.MACAT.COM.**

CRITICAL THINKING AND *COLLAPSE*

Primary critical thinking skill: INTERPRETATION
Secondary critical thinking skill: REASONING

American scholar Jared Diamond deploys his powers of interpretation to great effect in *Collapse: How Societies Choose to Fail or Survive* which seeks to understand the meaning behind the available evidence describing societies that have survived and those that have withered and died.

Why, for example, did the Norsemen of Scandinavia who colonized Greenland in the early tenth century not survive, while the inhabitants of Highland New Guinea did? With the evidence to hand, Diamond notes that a society's collapse tends to be preceded by a severe reduction in population and considerable decreases in political, economic and social complexity. Delving even deeper, Diamond isolates five major factors determine the success or failure of human societies in all periods of history: environmental degradation, which occurs when an ecosystem deteriorates as its resources are exhausted; climate change (natural or man-made); hostile neighbors; weakened trading partners; and access or otherwise to the resources that enable the society to adapt its challenges.

The breadth of Diamond's research provides the springboard from which to reach these definitions, but it inevitably also introduces complications; how can evidence produced by specialists in so many different disciplines be compared? Diamond's ability to understand the meaning of the evidence at hand – and his readiness to seek and supply clarifications of meaning where necessary – underpin his achievement, and comprise a textbook example of how interpretative skills can provide a framework for strong critical thinking.

ABOUT THE AUTHOR OF THE ORIGINAL WORK

Born in Boston in the United States in 1937, **Jared M. Diamond** studies human history using a wide-ranging multidisciplinary approach that draws on biology, anthropology, ecology, and geography. Diamond first trained as a biochemist at Harvard University and as a physiologist at Cambridge, but became interested in ecology when he visited New Guinea in 1964. He then developed an interest in environmental history, and is now professor of geography at the University of California, Los Angeles, as well as an environmental activist and popular writer. He won the prestigious Pulitzer Prize for his controversial 1997 work *Guns, Germs, and Steel.*

ABOUT THE AUTHOR OF THE ANALYSIS

Dr Rodolfo Maggio holds a masters degree in anthropology from the London School of Economics and a PhD in social anthropology from the University of Manchester. He is currently a postdoctoral researcher in the Department of Psychiatry at the University of Oxford.

ABOUT MACAT

GREAT WORKS FOR CRITICAL THINKING

Macat is focused on making the ideas of the world's great thinkers accessible and comprehensible to everybody, everywhere, in ways that promote the development of enhanced critical thinking skills.

It works with leading academics from the world's top universities to produce new analyses that focus on the ideas and the impact of the most influential works ever written across a wide variety of academic disciplines. Each of the works that sit at the heart of its growing library is an enduring example of great thinking. But by setting them in context – and looking at the influences that shaped their authors, as well as the responses they provoked – Macat encourages readers to look at these classics and game-changers with fresh eyes. Readers learn to think, engage and challenge their ideas, rather than simply accepting them.

'Macat offers an amazing first-of-its-kind tool for interdisciplinary learning and research. Its focus on works that transformed their disciplines and its rigorous approach, drawing on the world's leading experts and educational institutions, opens up a world-class education to anyone.'

Andreas Schleicher
Director for Education and Skills, Organisation for Economic Co-operation and Development

'Macat is taking on some of the major challenges in university education ... They have drawn together a strong team of active academics who are producing teaching materials that are novel in the breadth of their approach.'

Prof Lord Broers,
former Vice-Chancellor of the University of Cambridge

'The Macat vision is exceptionally exciting. It focuses upon new modes of learning which analyse and explain seminal texts which have profoundly influenced world thinking and so social and economic development. It promotes the kind of critical thinking which is essential for any society and economy. This is the learning of the future.'

Rt Hon Charles Clarke, former UK Secretary of State for Education

'The Macat analyses provide immediate access to the critical conversation surrounding the books that have shaped their respective discipline, which will make them an invaluable resource to all of those, students and teachers, working in the field.'

Professor William Tronzo, University of California at San Diego

WAYS IN TO THE TEXT

KEY POINTS

- Jared M. Diamond is a polymath* scholar—possessing a depth of knowledge in many fields of interest—whose work combines various parallel interests with an accessible narrative style. His approach has won him considerable if controversial fame across the world.

- Published in 2005, *Collapse: How Societies Choose to Fail or Survive* argues that societies fail because of five key factors; societies in many parts of the world today will also collapse, he argues, unless they learn lessons from those that survived.

- *Collapse* matters because it deals with global environmental issues and general patterns in human history, and because it has generated debate among academics.

Who Is Jared M. Diamond?

Jared M. Diamond, the author of *Collapse: How Societies Choose to Fail or Survive* (also sometimes subtitled *How Societies Choose to Fail or Succeed*), was born in 1937 in Boston, Massachusetts. His parents—his father was a pediatrician, his mother a teacher and concert pianist—were of Eastern European Jewish origin. Since his early years he has directed his inquisitive mind in multiple directions. For example, while his PhD at Cambridge University focused on the biophysics* and physiology* of membranes in the gall bladder (biophysics being the study of biological systems with methods borrowed from physics, physiology being the study of the functioning of living organisms),[1] he also conducted research in the ornithology* (study of birds) and ecology* (which examines the relationships between species and environment) of the South Pacific island of New Guinea.

In 1968 he was appointed professor of physiology at the medical school of the University of California, Los Angeles (UCLA). However, it is his interdisciplinary* approach (drawing on different academic disciplines) that laid the basis for his successful career. Ornithology taught him the value of comparing different populations that live in similar environments, a technique he later combined with his third research interest, environmental history.* This combination of environmental history and comparative methods* (systems requiring the examination of two or more cases to identify similarities and differences that might explain their respective outcomes) became a trademark, which he popularized with an accessible and storytelling-like writing style.

The formula proved extremely successful. Before, he had published only—though prolifically—in the fields of physiology, ecology, and ornithology.[2] Then, in the 1990s, he became more widely known following the publication of his books written for a popular audience. After his award-winning *The Third Chimpanzee* (1991), he received several prizes for *Guns, Germs, and Steel* (1997), including a Pulitzer Prize for General Nonfiction. *Collapse* (2005) is his fourth book.

What Does *Collapse* Say?

In *Collapse*, Diamond asks why some past civilizations experienced a severe reduction in population and considerable decreases in political, economic, and social complexity, before eventually collapsing. His answer is that they fell victim to one or more of the following five key factors: environmental degradation* (the decline of an ecosystem as a result of the progressive depletion of its resources), including overpopulation; changes in the climate;* hostile neighbors; weakened trading partners; and an absence of the cultural resources that enable a society to tackle these and other problems. He supports this general conclusion with a comparison between a set of historical civilizations, including the pre-Columbian Maya* of Mesoamerica (specifically what is today southeastern Mexico, Guatemala, Belize, the western part of El Salvador, and Honduras), the Norse (medieval Scandinavian) colonies of Greenland, the Polynesians of Henderson, Pitcairn, and Easter Islands, and the Anasazi* people of the American Southwest (the ancient inhabitants of the territory comprising contemporary southern Utah, northern Arizona, northwestern New Mexico, and southwestern Colorado).

The five key factors combined in different ways depending on their number and mutual influence. For example, all five contributed to the inexorable decline of the Norse colonies. Four out of five destroyed the Maya (no role was played by trade partners), and only three caused the collapse of the Anasazi—deforestation* (the removal of trees), a protracted drought, and the failure to solve the ensuing societal problems.

Diamond suggests that these same factors may undermine contemporary global societies, too, and even destroy them. For example, one or more of the five factors caused the recent fall of the African nations of Somalia and Rwanda,* and the former Yugoslavia, and are currently threatening countries such as Iraq and Indonesia. Even Australia and the United States are at risk, particularly from environmental damage, which is probably the single greatest threat to societies across the world.

Just a single factor can initiate the downward spiral of collapse. It happened in Easter Island, in the southeastern Pacific, where massive deforestation inadvertently caused a chain reaction leading to ecological and civilizational self-destruction. Similarly, pollution caused by global industrial powers potentially risks unsustainable damage.

Hence, *Collapse* urges readers to become conscious of the importance of human activities in shaping the future of civilizations, and to take corrective action against upcoming environmental catastrophes.

In the search for practical lessons that might help us to deal with our own problems, Diamond again looks at past civilizations. He analyzes cases in Japan of the Tokugawa* period (1603–1868), the Pacific island of Tikopia, and the New Guinea Highlands, and infers that ecological catastrophes can be avoided with a combination of restraint, increased knowledge, and axiological* flexibility—the ability of any given society to change its cultural values.

In contrast, other societies "chose" not to ensure their long-term sustainability, even if they were aware of their decline. For example, the Norse knew that their neighbors, the Inuit, were better able to cope with changes in the climate and other challenging factors. But their blind commitment to religion, their strong social cohesion, and their scorn for the Inuit (whom they regarded as inferior) prevented them from changing their values and learning from their neighbors. A similar kind of axiological rigidity, Diamond concludes, is also preventing contemporary global societies from making the choices that would promote *our* long-term sustainability.

Why Does *Collapse* Matter?

In *Collapse*, Diamond reaches conclusions that are relevant for one of the most controversial debates today: man-made climate change, its consequences, and the ways in which we should respond to it. In fact, he conceived the book precisely as an opportunity to learn from past societies that dealt with their environmental problems.

These preoccupations are motivated not only by the perceived risk of an upcoming catastrophe, but also by the lack of consensus regarding the extent and consequences of human-activated climate change. *Collapse* proves that such uncertainties and the ensuing political paralysis—immobilism*—is not new. There were societies in the past that, though aware of their decline, did not necessarily take steps to overcome it.

Indeed, Diamond contends that whether a society collapses or not largely depends on its cultural values and its political, economic, and social institutions. By producing factual evidence that human activities did change the course of distant societies, he intends to persuade us that our corrective action matters for us today just as much as it did for people in the past.

Unsurprisingly, *Collapse* proved an almost instant best seller and has been translated into 31 languages. Its success is clear evidence not just of the inherent and wide appeal of Diamond's subject matter, but of his talents as a popularizer of complex historical problems and their relevance to industrial societies today.

Readers appreciate not only the content of Diamond's work, but also his style of reasoning. With *Guns, Germs, and Steel*, a book based on the so-called "natural experiment"* (the study of a context exposed to influences beyond the control of the investigators, who try to demonstrate causal connections) and the comparison between societies that differ in time and space, he enjoyed similar strong sales. On the other hand, specialist academics around the world—especially anthropologists* (who study human beings), archaeologists* (who study past human activity), geographers, and historians—are very critical of these "popular" methodologies.

The ensuing controversy, however, proves that the book matters in the debate about how we can learn from previous societies. While specialists insist that there are irreducible differences between past and present, Diamond provides evidence that there are common elements, too. These commonalities are what make us human and, as such, they are of continuing relevance and importance.

NOTES

1   Jared M. Diamond, "Concentrating Activity of the Gall-bladder" (PhD diss., University of Cambridge, 1961).

2   See, for example: Jared M. Diamond et al., "Geophagy in New Guinea Birds," *Ibis* 141, no. 2 (1999): 181–93.

SECTION 1
INFLUENCES

THE AUTHOR AND THE HISTORICAL CONTEXT

KEY POINTS

- As in his previous work, in *Collapse* Diamond draws on the aims and methods of several academic disciplines to answer a question relevant for humanity at large: in this case, that of societal collapse.

- Diamond combined multiple interests, methods, and an accessible writing style into a unique blend that gained his books worldwide acclaim, notwithstanding much specialist criticism.

- Diamond's unique formula results from his career in physiology* (which looks at the functioning of biological systems) and ornithology* (the study of birds), his personal interest in anthropology* (which studies humankind) and the environment, and from his life experiences as a fieldworker and science writer.

Why Read This Text?

Jared M. Diamond's best-selling *Collapse: How Societies Choose to Fail or Survive* (2005) asks why some societies collapse and others do not. This is a typical "Diamondian" question, similar to the one he asked in his Pulitzer Prize-winning book *Guns, Germs, and Steel* (1997), where he asked why some societies come to dominate and others to be dominated. The way in which Diamond answers the question in *Collapse* is also typical of his argumentative style: a sweeping comparison between societies distant in space and time, observed as if they were "natural experiments"* (the observation of, say, a group of people in a given territory, exposed to influences beyond the control

> **❝** Ever since I was in my 20s and read Thor
> Heyerdahl's books about Easter Island, I became
> intrigued by the collapse of great societies—as are
> millions of other people. That interest has stayed with
> me over the last forty years, stimulated by visits to
> Maya ruins and Anasazi sites and by reading about
> other collapsed societies. I did not conceive of *Guns,
> Germs, and Steel* and *Collapse* as companion volumes
> from the start, but ... as soon as I came to think about
> what would be the subject of my next book, the
> answer became obvious: Collapse! **❞**
> Penguin Reader's Guide, "A Conversation with Jared Diamond"

of the investigators, in order to establish causal connections between those influences and any changes observed). Diamond also explains *Collapse*'s appeal in relation to his previous book, writing that: "many people … were looking out for my next book, but the other reason is that the subject of *Collapse* really grabs people."[1]

The "subject of *Collapse*" is societal collapse defined as a "drastic decrease in human population size and/or political/economic/social complexity, over a considerable area, for an extended time." This is a theme that Diamond had already addressed before the publication of *Collapse*.[2] In the book, he argues that different combinations of five factors caused and are causing the collapse of both past and present societies.

Diamond developed this intellectual style as an amalgamation of different disciplines he studied throughout his life. He began his intellectual career as a physiologist, developed a parallel interest in ornithology, then history, and eventually ethnography* (the study of groups of people, their customs, habits, and beliefs). His formula has been extremely successful, gaining him wide fame with his books written for a non-specialist audience. These include *The Third Chimpanzee* (1991),[3] *Guns, Germs, and Steel* (1997),[4] *The World Until Yesterday* (2012),[5] and *Why Is Sex Fun?* (1997),[6] *Collapse* is another milestone in this intellectual journey from the natural and physical sciences to social sciences and to popular science writing.

Author's Life

In 1937 Jared M. Diamond was born in Boston, Massachusetts, to a couple of Eastern European Jewish origin. Like his mother, he studied piano and became interested in teaching. Presumably influenced by his father, a pediatrician—a doctor specializing in children—Diamond obtained a PhD from Cambridge University on the physiology of membranes in the gall bladder.

At the same time, he developed an interest in ornithology and ecology* (the relationship between species and environment). He conducted research on the birds and environment of the Pacific island of New Guinea, and started to publish his findings. About this part of his life, he said: "Luckily my [academic] papers about birds were published in journals which no gall bladder physiologists ever read ... In academia, working in multiple fields is not a benefit but a penalty."[7]

Diamond developed a third line of investigation in environmental history* (the investigation of the relationship between human societies and the environment). He also began writing for a non-academic public. With his second book, *Guns, Germs, and Steel*, he achieved worldwide fame and was awarded a series of prizes. However, *Guns, Germs, and Steel* attracted fierce criticism, too. The book's conclusions gained him the reputation, among academics, of being a cultural imperialist* (one who imposes his or her own cultural values on others), an environmental determinist* (one who believes that the environment is the deciding factor for social outcomes), and a radical empiricist* (one who refuses to consider evidence that cannot be verified by observation).

In *Collapse,* Diamond seriously confronted those criticisms. Along with the radical empiricism of the natural experiment and the comparative method* (the analysis of different cases in order to identify similarities and differences that might explain differing outcomes), which he did not abandon, he enriched his research toolkit with the ethnographic methods of anthropology. It follows that his life has been underscored by a constant effort to answer general questions about humanity by blending the methods from different disciplines, notwithstanding the attacks of colleagues and critics.

Author's Background

Diamond's background deeply influenced his intellectual production. His doctoral studies in physiology convinced him of the value of isolating variables with the experimental method. He would later apply this method to study the history of relatively isolated societies, such as those of Tikopia and Easter Island in the Pacific. Later, his ornithological research in New Guinea required him to compare the environmental habitats of birds to understand the impact of a set of independent variables* (an expression borrowed from mathematics to indicate the external cause of a phenomenon). When he wrote his books, he used the same comparative methods to understand the evolution of human societies in relation to a set of independent variables—such as climate,* biodiversity,* fauna (animals), and continental axis.*

The intersection between experimental and comparative methods and Diamond's later interest in environmental history and in popularizing science resulted in his famous book *Guns, Germs, and Steel.* The book was widely acclaimed, but also made Diamond the target of much criticism, especially by anthropologists. In *Collapse*, Diamond tackles his critics head on by opening the book with a very ethnographic first chapter.

The chapter draws heavily on Diamond's own knowledge of Montana in the western United States. As a teenager, in the 1950s, he used to spend a few weeks of the summer in the state of Montana. His father prescribed medical treatment to a rancher's child, and a strong bond developed between the two families as a consequence.[8] Diamond later bought a house in Montana, which gave him even more opportunities to gain insights into the points of view of Montanans about the destiny of their territory.

Along with this insider perspective, in this chapter he compares several case studies of water, air, and soil pollution, as well as other major problems afflicting Montana today. So he uses ethnography, natural experiment, and the comparative method again. In conclusion, *Collapse* is not only a comparison of different societies, but also a synthesis of methodologies that Diamond has been refining throughout his whole life.

NOTES

1   Penguin Reader's Guide, "A Conversation with Jared Diamond," penguin. com, n.d., accessed September 9, 2015, www.penguin.com/read/book-clubs/collapse/9780143117001.

2   Jared M. Diamond, "The Last Americans: Environmental Collapse and the End of Civilization," *Harper's Magazine*, June 2003; Diamond, "Easter's End," *Discover Magazine*, August 1995; Diamond, "Paradise Lost," *Discover Magazine*, November 1997.

3   Jared M. Diamond, *The Third Chimpanzee: The Evolution and Future of the Human Animal* (London: HarperCollins, 2006).

4   Jared M. Diamond, *Guns, Germs, and Steel* (London: Random House, 2013).

5   Jared M. Diamond, *The World Until Yesterday: What Can We Learn from Traditional Societies?* (New York: Viking, 2013).

6   Jared M. Diamond, *Why Is Sex Fun?: The Evolution of Human Sexuality* (London: Hachette, 2014).

7   Gillian Tett, "The Science Interview: Jared Diamond," *Financial Times*, October 11, 2013, accessed September 30, 2015, www.ft.com/intl/cms/s/2/1f786618-307a-11e3-80a4-00144feab7de.html#axzz3jQUrhdub.

8   Jared M. Diamond, *Collapse: How Societies Choose to Fail or Survive* (London: Penguin, 2011), 27.

MODULE 2
ACADEMIC CONTEXT

KEY POINTS

- Diamond has not necessarily discovered something new. Rather, his innovation consists in analyzing and presenting existing material in novel ways.

- The study of the relationship between human societies and the environment began with a school of thought called "environmental determinism"* (the theory that the environment determines the historical trajectories of a society associated with a particular territory), with which Diamond is closely associated.

- In writing *Collapse*, Diamond was influenced by his predecessors to the extent that he used existing data on past collapses both to engage with and expand on previous theories of societal collapse.

The Work in its Context

Before Jared M. Diamond's *Collapse: How Societies Choose to Fail or Survive* was published, the theme of societal collapse had been explored by the anthropologist* Norman Yoffee* and the anthropologist and archaeologist* George Cowgill,*[1] as well as by the archaeologist and anthropologist Brian Fagan,*[2] and the anthropologist and historian Joseph Tainter.*[3] In the 1990s, researchers became increasingly interested in accounting for societal collapse with environmental explanations. For example, in a 1995 article published in *Nature*, David A. Hodell,* Jason H. Curtis,* and Mark Brenner,* a team of researchers with different specialisms in the natural sciences, argued that a shift toward drier climate* conditions accelerated the collapse of the pre-Columbian Maya* people (a civilization that occupied the

> ❝ Most geographers think of the theory of environmental determinism as a musty, fusty relic of the past. But most geographers do not pay much attention to the best-seller lists. ❞
>
> James M. Blaut, "Environmentalism and Eurocentrism"

area of what is today southeastern Mexico, Guatemala, Belize, the western part of El Salvador, and Honduras from some 4,000 years ago).[4] It is from these studies that Diamond forms his synthesis in order to draw lessons for today.

The environmental historian* John R. McNeill* explains that "environmental historians have normally resisted the urge" of "combing the past for episodes that provide salutary lessons for the present."[5] In contrast, Diamond proposes that history be considered as a science that produces laws, allows predictions, and can be instructive about current affairs. Even though it is impossible to create laboratory conditions* in these fields (unlike chemistry or physics), the so-called "natural experiment"* is possible. This consists of comparing different, non-laboratory-bound cases in which a potentially key variable is absent or present.

For example, you can note that Easter Island and Mayan societies collapsed while experiencing environmental damage. From this you can postulate that environmental damage is a major cause of collapse. However, a correlation between collapse and environment should be drawn while taking differences into account. In this case, it is determining that Easter Island was an isolated island in the middle of the Pacific, and that the Mayan Empire was anything but isolated or peripheral. This difference highlights that isolation is not a necessary condition for collapse but a dispensable cause.

Overview of the Field

At the beginning of the twentieth century, environmental determinism was the prevailing theory in geography. It dates back to the thinkers of ancient Greece, such as the philosophers Plato* and Aristotle* and the physician Hippocrates,* and to later philosophers such as Montesquieu,* active in the eighteenth century, who asserted that environmental factors cause racial, cultural, social, and moral differences between populations. Environmental determinism can be summarized as follows: "Cold northern climates produce hardy and thrifty people" whereas "the unrelenting heat along the equator produces lazy people."[6]

Environmental determinism was opposed by the American geographer Carl O. Sauer* and other so-called "cultural possibilists"*[7] in the 1920s; for them, the approach reduced human beings to mere subjects of the environment, and was therefore unable to account for human modifications of the environment itself. They proposed, instead, a cultural perspective to understand the relationship between people and the environment. However, the application of these ideas was complicated by the controversial definition of culture, something that has been the subject of endless debate. Culture was initially considered to be synonymous with civilization; this idea was criticized for measuring all cultures from less to more civilized. So a new tendency to define each different culture according to its own values, beliefs, and practices emerged. In the search for unifying underlying principles, scholars later began to examine the elementary structures of each culture. Culture was looked at as a particular discourse from which it was possible to extract a sort of grammar. But this approach was seen as unable to account for human initiative and change. Ultimately, no single definition of culture is unanimously accepted.[8]

From the 1960s, culture was seen as the product of the systemic interaction between human beings and the environment (that is, the interactions inside a system defined, in this case, by people and the environment).[9] Then, the anthropologists Andrew P. Vayda* and Bonnie J. McCay* proposed a focus on individual behavior to identify the specific paths of systemic interactions.[10] Subsequently, a more structural approach was introduced to frame these individual paths within the broader setting of political and ideological forces.

These different perspectives are not discussed in *Collapse*. Rather than addressing a specific debate in the field of human–environment relationships, Diamond stepped into the discussion with a modified version of the environmental determinist position. Instead of explaining human societies as a mere consequence of their different environmental conditions, Diamond theorized a complex interlocking of multiple factors, including culture, politics, and even chance.

Academic Influences

Diamond was aware of previous attempts by other scholars to explain the causes of societal collapse. For example, in *The Collapse of Complex Societies* (1988), the anthropologist Joseph Tainter argues that societies collapse after reaching an unsustainable degree of complexity because they are unable to produce enough organizational and physical energy to support their hypertrophic*—excessively, unsustainably grown— structure.[11]

To reach this conclusion, Tainter compared three cases of collapse: the Western Roman Empire, the Maya civilization, and the Anasazi* culture of the southwestern United States, an approach that resembles Diamond's own comparative method. Tainter, however, concluded that collapse is a feature of all societies, whereas Diamond, on the basis of a larger sample of cases, argues that some societies avoid that kind of crisis.

Diamond is also familiar with "Population Crises and Population Cycles," a work by the British scholars William M. S. Russell* and Claire Russell,* who, like Tainter, argue that societies are structurally responsible for their crises.[12] Crises, for the Russells, depend on the differential growth of the population and the resources to support it. Societies can relieve the pressure of a growing population only with measures such as birth control. Examples recalled in this study are borrowed from China, West Africa, western Asia, the northern Mediterranean, and northwest Europe. Diamond himself mentions birth control as a prudent measure taken by the people of the southwest Pacific island of Tikopia to avoid the collapse of their society. However, he does not consider population growth as the only or main cause of societal collapse. Rather, his argument is that there are multiple causes, and that a major role is played by the environment.

These studies influenced Diamond to the extent that they provided him with a larger set of case studies. In terms of theory, he does not necessarily argue against Tainter's theory that societies have a tendency to collapse. Rather, he makes the additional point that they can survive their crises if corrective measures are taken in time. Similarly, the theory that collapse is caused by the differential growth of a population and the resources to support it is actually part of Diamond's own reasoning about the collapse of the African state of Rwanda.*

NOTES

1   Norman Yoffee and George Cowgill, eds., *The Collapse of Ancient States and Civilizations* (Tucson: University of Arizona Press, 1988).

2   Brian Fagan, *Floods, Famines, and Emperors: El Niño and the Fate of Civilizations* (New York: Basic Books, 1999).

3   Joseph Tainter, *The Collapse of Complex Societies* (Cambridge: Cambridge University Press, 1988).

4   David A. Hodell et al., "Possible Role of Climate in the Collapse of Classic Maya Civilization," *Nature* 375, no. 6530 (1995): 391–4.

5   John R. McNeill, "A Usable Past," *American Scientist* 93, no. 2 (2005): 172.

6   David Correia, "F**k Jared Diamond," *Capitalism Nature Socialism* 24, no. 4 (2013): 1–6.

7   Gabriel Judkins et al., "Determinism within Human–Environment Research and the Rediscovery of Environmental Causation," *The Geographical Journal* 174, no. 1 (2008): 17–29.

8   See: Tim Ingold, "Introduction to Culture," in *Companion Encyclopedia of Anthropology*, ed. Tim Ingold (London and New York: Routledge, 1994), 329–49.

9   Karl W. Butzer, "Cultural Ecology," in *Geography in America*, ed. Gary L. Gaile and Cort J. Willmott (Columbus: Merrill, 1989), 192–208; Marvin Harris, *Cultural Materialism: The Struggle for a Science of Culture* (New York: Random House, 1979); Roy A. Rappaport, *Pigs for the Ancestors: Ritual in the Ecology of a New Guinea People* (New Haven: Yale University Press,1968).

10 Andrew P. Vayda and Bonnie J. McCay, "New Directions in Ecology and Ecological Anthropology," *Annual Review of Anthropology* 4 (1975): 293–306.

11 Tainter, *Collapse of Complex Societies*.

12 Claire Russell and William M. S. Russell, "Population Crises and Population Cycles," *Medicine, Conflict and Survival* 16, no. 4 (2000): 383–410.

MODULE 3
THE PROBLEM

KEY POINTS

- At the core of Diamond's works *Guns, Germs, and Steel* and *Collapse* are questions about the fate of human societies and of the right way to study the history of human societies.

- Participants in the debate criticize both *Collapse* and previous works by Diamond for similar reasons, including environmental determinism* (the belief that it is environment, exclusively, that decides society and social outcomes), and for blaming past civilizations for their own collapses.

- The contemporary debate is dominated by accusations of environmental determinism and Western imperialism* (the ideology justifying the rule of European powers over large territories in Africa, Oceania, and the Americas). Rather than questioning the overall conclusions of *Collapse*, participants in the discussion question Diamond's ideological, methodological, and theoretical approaches.

Core Question

At the core of Jared M. Diamond's *Collapse: How Societies Choose to Fail or Survive* is a question about the cause of all societal collapses. By comparing a series of modern and ancient case studies, Diamond argues that all societal collapses result from a combination of the same five factors. He proposes that modern societies collapse because they are unable to solve the same kind of problems faced by those in the past. Diamond intended this theory to be valid for all societies past, present, and future. He calls the method with which he achieved such

> ❝ Diamond won a Pulitzer Prize because he made this ridiculous, racist argument sound like common sense. His books do not merely sanitize a history of colonial violence; they are its disinfectant. ❞
>
> David Correia, "F**k Jared Diamond"

a comprehensive theory "comparative environmental history."* This is the same kind of approach he used for his previous book *Guns, Germs, and Steel*.[1] It follows that *Collapse* is not only a book about societal failures but also a confirmation of Diamond's belief in this method.

Guns, Germs, and Steel was criticized for using this approach. Critics found it excessively simplistic to determine the fate of human societies in environmental terms. A more comprehensive explanation of the relationship between society and history, in their view, needs to take into account power relations and other human activities, rather than the supposedly all-encompassing influence of the environment.

In *Guns*, however, Diamond was not necessarily as simplistic as his critics argued. The title of the book itself listed three concurring causes; if he used the same kind of approach to answer the question posed in *Collapse* (that is, a multiplicity of factors and the prominent role played by the environment), it is because he was persuaded it was sound. It follows that at the core of *Collapse* there is not only a question about the fate of human societies but also a certain reaffirmation of Diamond's method for studying them.

The Participants

Theorists of societal collapse, such as the American anthropologist* and historian Joseph Tainter* and the British scholars William M. S.* and Claire Russell,* are among the main academic influences on *Collapse*. Rather than arguing against or in favor of their theories,

Diamond drew on their and other studies of societal collapses to formulate his own theory. It follows that the debate in which Diamond took part was less about the ultimate causes of collapse and more about which approach better suited the study of human societies.

Participants in this debate included many of the critics of Diamond's earlier works. For example, anthropologists writing on the *Savage Mind* website questioned the soundness of Diamond's approach to studying human societies, especially its ethical consequences. They were particularly critical because they regarded Diamond's approach as the basis of a determinist argument, even a demonstration of Western superiority.[2]

They identified such environmental determinist logic in *Guns, Germs, and Steel*. The book argued that European societies dominated other societies (especially Native Americans, Indigenous Australians, and Africans) because 13,000 years ago Europeans were favored by biogeographic factors, such as a milder climate,* continental axis* (an imaginary line traced horizontally on a continent whose territory extends for longer from east to west than from north to south), and a larger number of plants and animals capable of being domesticated. *Savage Mind* bloggers saw this approach as based on the assumption that, given a better head start, any society would necessarily develop such fundamentals of all settled states as agriculture and metallurgy earlier than less favored societies. It followed that Diamond's approach was seen to reduce the diverse fates of human societies to the mere influence of the environment.

However, the major consequences of the environmental determinist premise of Diamond's argument were also questioned. In the critics' view, arguing that the environment is the ultimate reason why societies develop in one way or another amounts to an implicit justification for European invasion, domination, and colonialism: in other words, Europeans dominated because they were better served by their environmental conditions; had Native Americans, Indigenous

Australians, or Africans been blessed with better environments they would have dominated instead.

The Contemporary Debate

Unconvinced by the criticism, Diamond insisted that environmental and ecological factors have a crucial impact on human history and culture. At the same time, he did not deny that cultural and historical factors and even individual choices play a role in shaping the destiny of human societies. The correct approach, for Diamond, lies somewhere between these two extremes:

- geographic and environmental explanations based on detailed technical facts
- taking the role of history and culture into account.

The influence of the contemporary debate can be clearly identified in *Collapse*. In the book, Diamond directly addressed the issue of determinism (the belief that every event has a predetermined cause),[3] reductionism (the explanation of a phenomenon in relation to a relatively small number of factors, and even to a single factor),[4] and of holding societies responsible for their own destiny.[5] Simultaneously, he enriched his methodological toolkit with the ethnographic* methods typically adopted by anthropologists, his most fierce critics. For example, in the first chapter about ecological problems in Montana, he uses ethnography to complement his theory of societal collapse with a wealth of fine-grained details from the everyday life of contemporary Montanans.

Furthermore, he tried to balance his search for synthetic answers with an appreciation of the complications. In this respect, he said: "When I began to plan this book, I didn't appreciate those complications, and I naively thought that the book would just be about environmental damage ... I learned that there is no case of a pure environmental collapse."[6] The outcome of Diamond coming to terms with the criticisms is the five-point framework he arrived at in *Collapse*. Rather than a determinist argument that explains the fate of all societies in terms of environmental conditions, this theory takes multiple aspects into consideration. However, that has not necessarily placated his critics.

NOTES

1   Jared M. Diamond, *Guns, Germs, and Steel* (London: Random House, 2013).

2   Kerim Friedman, "From the Archives: Savage Minds vs. Jared Diamond," *Savage Minds*, January 22, 2012, accessed September 30, 2015, http://savageminds.org/2012/01/22/from-the-archives-savage-minds-vs-jared-diamond/.

3   Jared M. Diamond, *Collapse: How Societies Choose to Fail or Survive* (London: Penguin, 2011) 20.

4   Diamond, *Collapse*, 304.

5   Diamond, *Collapse*, 324.

6   Amos Esty, "An Interview with Jared Diamond," *American Scientist Online*, n.d., accessed September 30, 2015, www.americanscientist.org/bookshelf/pub/jared-diamond.

MODULE 4
THE AUTHOR'S CONTRIBUTION

KEY POINTS

- Although Jared Diamond has answered the questions posed in *Collapse* with a well-organized and evidence-based set of answers, whether these answers are satisfactory is a matter of personal judgment.

- Diamond labels his method as "comparative environmental history,"* which consists of comparing in-depth case studies of different societies in order to isolate key variables that provide general explanations.

- *Collapse* does not constitute an innovation in terms of theory, content, or method. Rather, it is innovative in the way it synthesizes an unprecedented quantity of case studies on societal collapse.

Author's Aims

Jared M. Diamond pursued four main objectives in writing *Collapse: How Societies Choose to Fail or Survive.* First, he sought to answer the question of why some civilizations collapse while others solve the problems confronting them and prosper. Second, he attempted to establish similarities between the collapses of different civilizations. Third, he discussed how it is possible to draw lessons for the present from the fate of those societies that survived and those that collapsed. Fourth, and most importantly, he said he wrote *Collapse* to raise awareness of current global environmental problems and to warn against the risks of underestimating the signs of our possible upcoming collapse.

Diamond began with an ethnographic* description of environmental problems in Montana, before moving on to a collection

> **❝** And so what I actually did for 45 years, although it wasn't geography or history, was good unplanned preparation for my present career in geography and history. **❞**
>
> Jared Diamond, "About Me," www.jareddiamond.org

of case studies that illustrate the causes that led a set of selected societies to collapse and others to survive. Past societies are compared with contemporary societies that have either collapsed or undergone crisis management. On the basis of this broad comparison of past and present, collapsed and survived societies, Diamond drew a set of practical lessons for us today.

While Diamond's argument is supported by detailed case studies, some of the studies he quoted (for example, the study of deforestation* in Chaco Canyon in the southwestern United States) have been questioned on the grounds of inaccuracy, which might undermine the solidity of his views. Furthermore, although the book did contribute to making the debate about environmentalism more visible and relevant, it has been argued that Diamond's distinction between "bad" business and businesses that want to protect the environment did a favor to many powerful companies responsible for many of today's environmental problems.[1]

Approach

Diamond labels his approach "comparative environmental history," a system that combines methodologies borrowed from biology, geography, and history, and which includes radiocarbon dating* (a method for dating objects through the analysis of radioactive markers), archaeological* and botanical* surveys, and pollen and charcoal analysis* (a method that determines the presence of species of plants in a given territory through the analysis of their remains) and the like.

For example, his argument that Easter Island collapsed is supported by analyses of pollen sediments (providing evidence of deforestation) combined with studies of animal bones in garbage dumps (suggesting a decrease in food resources). These analyses are then compared with those conducted in other sites.

He outlined this multidisciplinary* and comparative approach to the study of history in *Natural Experiments of History,* a collection of seven case studies he coedited with the economist and political scientist James Robinson.*[2] The book explains that, although it is not possible to treat societies as if they were bacteria on a Petri dish, comparing in-depth studies of similar societies whose environmental variables differ might provide a general explanation for their fates.

For example, in the southwestern Pacific, the island of Tikopia was able to support a population of 1,200 people for more than 3,000 years thanks to the micromanagement of resources and to birth control. Similarly, Icelanders learned how to avoid soil degradation, enabling them to reach one of the highest per capita incomes* in the world. Though very distant and different, these societies have something in common: they learned how to extract resources from their environment without destroying it.

About the comparative method, Diamond wrote: "I have belabored this necessity for both good individual studies and good comparisons, because scholars practicing one approach too often belittle the contributions of the other approach ... Only from the weight of evidence provided by a comparative study of many societies with different outcomes can one hope to reach convincing conclusions."[3] This approach is not necessarily innovative in anthropology,* although it is less popular than in-depth, long-term ethnography.

Contribution in Context

It is not easy to evaluate *Collapse* as a contribution to a single field. Rather, it contributes to many, including anthropology, archaeology, and history, for it has been questioned by scholars in each of these fields. Diamond does not directly address previous theoretical works on the theme of civilizational collapse (such as those by scholars such as Joseph Tainter[*4] and William M. S. Russell[*] and Claire Russell[*]).[5] Instead, he develops an argument on the basis of a comparison of case studies.

In terms of theory building, *Collapse* is an unprecedented synthesis of an unparalleled quantity of case studies of societal collapse. It includes previous analysis of collapsed societies, embraces previous theories of societal collapse, and expands them so as to include the totality of possible combinations of collapse factors. As such, the book makes a considerable contribution to, for example, the anthropologist and historian Joseph Tainter's theory of structural collapse (according to which cultures collapse after reaching an unsustainable degree of complexity, being unable to produce enough organizational and physical energy to support their overdeveloped structure). However, Diamond's theory is not revolutionary to the extent that it draws almost entirely on preexisting material.

With regard to content, *Collapse* is not based on firsthand data; instead it looks to previous in-depth studies. For example, the two chapters about the collapse of the Norse (that is, premodern Scandinavian) colonies overlap partly with the work of Thomas McGovern,[*] who specializes in climate and island archaeology.[6] To take another example, the equation between the fates of Easter Island and the Earth was advanced by the archaeologist Paul Bahn[*] and by John Flenley,[*] an expert in the analysis of ancient particles of dust. So to the extent that *Collapse* does not say much that was not already there, it is not seen as a groundbreaking contribution to the study of societal collapse.

In terms of methodology, Diamond followed the steps of previous comparative studies of societal collapse. For example, Joseph Tainter compared the fate of the Western Roman Empire, the Maya[*] civilization, and the north American Anasazi[*] culture, and argued that they collapsed because of a decrease in their social complexity.[7] Diamond agrees with the methodology, but expands it to include and synthesize a larger quantity of case studies. Consequently, he achieves different, more far-reaching conclusions.

NOTES

1 Stephanie McMillan, "The Buying and Selling of Jared Diamond," counterpunch.org, December 12, 2009, accessed September 9, 2015, www.counterpunch.org/2009/12/08/the-buying-and-selling-of-jared-diamond/.

2 Jared M. Diamond and James A. Robinson, eds., *Natural Experiments of History* (Cambridge, MA: Harvard University Press, 2010).

3 Jared M. Diamond, *Collapse: How Societies Choose to Fail or Survive* (London: Penguin, 2011), 17.

4 Joseph Tainter, *The Collapse of Complex Societies* (Cambridge: Cambridge University Press, 1988).

5 Claire Russell and William M. S. Russell, "Population Crises and Population Cycles," *Medicine, Conflict and Survival* 16, no. 4 (2000): 383–410.

6 Thomas McGovern et al., "Northern Islands, Human Error, and Environmental Degradation: A View of Social and Ecological Change in the Medieval North Atlantic," *Human Ecology* 16 (1988).

7 Tainter, *Collapse of Complex Societies.*

SECTION 2
IDEAS

MODULE 5
MAIN IDEAS

KEY POINTS

- Jared M. Diamond says a combination of five key factors causes human civilizations to collapse. The most important is the fifth: a society's ability to respond to the other four factors.

- Diamond takes examples from past societies to illustrate why some succumbed because of the five factors, and why some were able to survive their crises.

- Diamond finds a balance between a scientific and accessible language with a storytelling approach to scientific writing that captures readers as it informs them.

Key Themes

In *Collapse: How Societies Choose to Fail or Survive*, Jared M. Diamond suggests that a combination of five key factors causes human civilizations to collapse. The first factor is environmental degradation,* including deforestation,* pollution, soil depletion, erosion* (the movement of soil and rock from one place to another as a result of rain, wind, agriculture, and deforestation) and overpopulation. The extent of such degradation depends on two environmental subfactors: fragility (susceptibility to damage) and resilience (potential for recovery). These subfactors, in turn, depend on people—who cut trees, for example, or catch fish at sustainable* or unsustainable rates—and the environment itself, which is either more or less capable of sustaining human action.

The second factor is climate change,* which has historically been natural but is today caused by human action, and consists of long-term

> **❝** For the first time in history, we face the risk of a global decline. But we also are the first to enjoy the opportunity of learning quickly from developments in societies anywhere else in the world today, and from what has unfolded in societies at any time in the past. That's why I wrote this book. **❞**
>
> Jared M. Diamond, *Collapse: How Societies Choose to Fail or Survive*

and large-scale variations in rainfall, temperature, humidity, and the like. Hotter, colder, wetter, drier, or more or less variable climates cause drought, unbearable temperatures, reduced crop yields, and food shortages. For example, a severe drought hit the Maya,* in the area that today is Mexico, Guatemala, Belize, the western part of El Salvador, and Honduras, and the Anasazi* of the American Southwest; similarly, the Norse ("Viking") colonies in Greenland were unable to survive the Little Ice Age*—a cold period of climatic history between about 1400 and 1800.

The third factor is increased hostility by neighboring groups. Indeed, "collapses for ecological or other reasons often masquerade as military defeats."[1]

The fourth is the reverse of the third, the withdrawal of support and trade from friendly neighbors. Indeed, most societies "depend to some extent on friendly neighbors ... for imports of essential trade goods."[2]

The fifth factor is a society's ability to respond to its problems. While the four factors above may or may not prove significant for a particular collapse, the fifth factor has always and everywhere proved crucial.

The key lesson is, therefore, that even if societies perceive their problems, they are not necessarily able to solve them. Whether a society is able to counter any of the above factors, or a combination of the four, largely depends on its cultural values and its political, economic, and social institutions.

Exploring the Ideas

Diamond takes examples from past societies to illustrate why some succumbed because of the five factors and some were able to survive.

Easter Island in the southeast Pacific is an example of collapse caused by the first factor. Society there fell because all of the palm trees were chopped down to make canoes and rollers to transport their *moai:* the giant statues dotted around the island. The people did not know that this particular type of palm would not recover as fast as the palms of other Polynesian islands. In addition, the island chiefs competed for self-promotion and pushed the logging activity to the point of no return. As a consequence, the island fauna (animals) died out, the agricultural system soon proved insufficient to feed the entire population, and they eventually turned to internal warfare and cannibalism. Easter Island, Diamond concludes, "is as close as we can get to a 'pure' ecological collapse, in this case due to total deforestation."[3]

The Norse colonies of Greenland, to take a different example, collapsed as a result of all five factors—but especially because the Scandinavian colonists were unable to change their values and take corrective action. For them, "it was out of the question to invest less in churches, to imitate or intermarry with the Inuit, and thereby to face an eternity in Hell just in order to survive another winter on Earth."[4] Ultimately, it is such a rigidity of values that caused their collapse.

In contrast, three examples of societies that overcame deforestation, erosion, and soil infertility illustrate the importance of flexibility and corrective action.

At the beginning of seventeenth century, the Tokugawa* shoguns of Japan—the ruling elite—tackled deforestation with the imposition of resource management policies even though that meant less wood was available for their spectacular palaces. And the Highlanders of

Papua New Guinea used their botanical* knowledge—their study of plants—to increase soil fertility and reforestation* when a wood crisis followed the growth of the farming population about 7,000 years ago.

The chiefs of the island of Tikopia, apart from their regular micromanagement of food production, took the bitter decision at some point in 1600 C.E. to exterminate their highly valued pigs because they were destroying their crops. This action was taken even though, as Diamond writes, "pigs are the sole large domestic animal and a principal status symbol of Melanesian societies."[5] Unlike their Easter Island counterparts, these chiefs valued their survival more than their status.

Language and Expression

The main stylistic challenge in *Collapse,* as in other books by Diamond, is finding the right balance between scientific and accessible language. In order to support his conclusions, Diamond has to include a wealth of technical details borrowed from the fields of geography, anthropology,* archaeology,* and botany. He is aware that the average layperson and even the student might lack the necessary knowledge to keep all these details in mind and, simultaneously, follow the overall argument. Thus, Diamond balances the amount of technicalities with a series of anecdotes that exemplify a point.

For example, as an illustration of the fifth factor, he writes, "What did the Easter Islander who cut the last palm tree say while he was doing it?"[6] To express the concept of resource management, he tells us, "As my Norwegian archaeologist friend Christian Keller expressed it, 'Life in Greenland is all about finding the good patches of useful resources.'"[7] Here, the "Malthusian trap"* is important; this is the English economist Thomas Malthus's theory that the exponential growth of human beings tends to surpass food production. Referencing this idea, Diamond discusses the Rwandan* genocide (in the course of which some 500,000–1,000,000 people, largely of the Tutsi ethnic group, were murdered by members of the Hutu ethnic group), noting, "Friends of mine who visited Rwanda in 1984 sensed an ecological disaster in the making."[8]

The repeated use of "friends" from distant places has at least three major outcomes. First, it puts "a personal face on a subject that could otherwise seem abstract."[9] Second, it makes the reader feel much closer to issues that would otherwise feel foreign, distant, and perhaps even irrelevant. Third, it presents the search for scientific knowledge more like a worldwide conversation among "friends," rather than a painstaking debate between nitpicking specialists gathered in an ivory tower.

In this way, he creates a sort of scientific storytelling that captures readers at the same time as it educates them.

NOTES

1   Jared M. Diamond, *Collapse: How Societies Choose to Fail or Survive* (London: Penguin, 2011), 11.

2   Diamond, *Collapse*, 12.

3   Diamond, *Collapse*, 18.

4   Diamond, *Collapse*, 247.

5   Diamond, *Collapse*, 521.

6   Diamond, *Collapse*, 112.

7   Diamond, *Collapse*, 210.

8   Diamond, *Collapse*, 318.

9   Diamond, *Collapse*, 30.

MODULE 6
SECONDARY IDEAS

KEY POINTS

*   Although contemporary global societies are threatened by the same kind of factors that destroyed past civilizations, they are in a better position to face these challenges.

*   Diamond takes examples from contemporary and past societies to illustrate that they face similar challenges, and to draw lessons on how to avoid the risk of collapse.

*   Even though past societies were deeply damaged by five key factors associated with social collapse, some did not disappear entirely. While Diamond did not explore this resilience, he looked at why some societies survived.

Other Ideas

After establishing the main factors causing societies to fail, in *Collapse: How Societies Choose to Fail or Survive*, Jared M. Diamond seeks to demonstrate that it is possible to draw parallels between past and present societies. These parallels suggest that as long as societies are subject to the same processes, they also share the same fates. The result is that they allow us to predict the collapse of contemporary global societies.

Present and past societies share many problems of environmental degradation* (Diamond's first factor): "The processes through which past societies have undermined themselves by damaging their environments fall into eight categories, whose relative importance differs from case to case: deforestation* and habitat destruction; soil problems (erosion,* salinization,* and soil fertility losses); water management* problems; overhunting; overfishing; the impact of

> ❝ But there are also differences between the modern
> world and its problems, and those past societies and
> their problems. We shouldn't be so naïve as to think
> that study of the past will yield simple solutions, directly
> transferable to our societies today. ❞
>
> Jared M. Diamond, *Collapse: How Societies Choose to Fail or Survive*

introduced species on native species; human population growth; and
the increased human impact as disposable incomes rise."[1]

Further, Diamond highlights important differences, which
encourage us to consider innovative solutions to avoid the collapse of
contemporary global societies. "The environmental problems facing
us today include the same eight that undermined past societies, plus
four new ones: human-caused climate change,* buildUp of toxic
chemicals in the environment, energy shortages, and full human
utilization of the Earth's photosynthetic capacity."*[2] Globalization*—
the increasing convergence of political, economic, and social ties across
continents—is responsible for the four additional problems.

Globalization is also part of the solution, however: "We also are the
first to enjoy the opportunity of learning quickly from developments
in societies anywhere else in the world today, and from what has
unfolded in societies at any time in the past."[3] Here Diamond is
implicitly saying that his writing the book is itself an example of the
kind of capacity for reflection on the past that distinguishes modern
society from that of the Easter Islanders, for instance.

Exploring the Ideas
Diamond argues that the problems faced by societies in the past and
those faced by contemporary societies can be generally grouped into
the same categories: the five key factors.

For example, the Norse ("Vikings") exhausted their irreplaceable resources of turf to build houses and to burn as fuel. This played an important part in their collapse. Similarly, the United States, China, and other contemporary societies are currently consuming an unsustainable quantity of fuel. Fuel exhaustion will arguably cause, at least in part, the collapse of societies unable to find alternative sources of energy.

To take another example, Easter Islanders pursued the increase in their chiefdoms'* status by building large statues at the expense of their forests. Similarly, industrialized societies seem unable to refrain from increasing their rates of production, even though they live on a planet with finite resources.

Easter Islanders could not rely on trade partners. Similarly, inhabitants of Earth cannot seek the support of other planets. Hence, we should value our resources higher than our production.

We can look to the past for solutions to the problems faced by contemporary societies; the Japanese shoguns of the Tokugawa* period (1603–1868) avoided a self-inflicted deforestation thanks to their awareness of the risks and their willingness to impose measures to manage their forests. Similarly, thanks to the imposition of environmental policies by two dictators, Rafael Trujillo* and Joaquin Balaguer,* the Dominican Republic avoided the environmental degradation experienced throughout the nineteenth and twentieth centuries by its neighbor Haiti.

Whether we will be able to avoid our own collapse largely depends on our capacity to tackle the 12 environmental problems identified by Diamond. Further, he argues that it is possible to recognize signs both of hope and of despair; he says some modern businesses "are among the most environmentally destructive forces today, while others provide some of the most effective environmental protection."[4] As in the past, these powerful players might choose to pursue their own goals at the expense of society or at sustainable rates.

Overlooked

One aspect that has been overlooked in *Collapse* is Diamond's acknowledgment that collapse and survival often coexist. In the book, he generally places more emphasis on the collapse of societies rather than the survival of their vestiges or people. This is perhaps unsurprising, and legitimate, given that his is a book about collapse rather than survival or resilience. However, Diamond did recognize that some people survived the collapse of their societies. For example, he noted that the extinct North American Anasazi* people did not entirely vanish and that their descendants currently inhabit contemporary Native American societies.[5]

Diamond's recognition that a degree of resilience is present in collapsed societies has not been given much academic credence. For example, the anthropologists Patricia McAnany* and Norman Yoffee* argued that Diamond's failure to recognize that no society simply disappears severely undermines his argument.[6] It is true that Diamond dealt only with the descendants of the Anasazi and other collapsed societies briefly and did not further analyze their persistence—but it is important, however, that he has at least mentioned their survival, as this balances a view of collapse as extreme population decline and loss of culture with an image of endurance and adaptation.

McAnany and Yoffee criticized Diamond for underestimating societal resilience. For example, to oppose his argument about the collapse of the Maya Empire, they argued that even though some Maya cities were dramatically depopulated in the eighth and ninth centuries, the population of other regions of the Mayan Empire simultaneously increased. Furthermore, people of Maya descent lived in the populous cities of the postclassic* period of the region's history (about 950–1539), and seven million people currently inhabit contemporary Mexico and northern Central America.

If adequately combined, the concept of collapse and resilience would potentially grant a much deeper theoretical understanding of human societies. It might be argued, for instance, that collapses are processes of destructive creation in which societies undergo a redefinition of their relationship with the environment through the development of a new culture.

NOTES

1   Jared M. Diamond, *Collapse: How Societies Choose to Fail or Survive* (London: Penguin, 2011), 4.

2   Diamond, *Collapse*, 5.

3   Diamond, *Collapse*, 11.

4   Diamond, *Collapse*, 11.

5   Diamond, *Collapse*, 135.

6   Patricia A. McAnany and Norman Yoffee, eds., *Questioning Collapse: Human Resilience, Ecological Vulnerability, and the Aftermath of Empire* (New York: Cambridge University Press, 2010).

MODULE 7
ACHIEVEMENT

KEY POINTS

- While Diamond's argument in *Collapse* is not necessarily revolutionary, the book has a number of merits, for which it has been praised.

- *Collapse*'s most important achievement is to provide an evidence-based argument in support of an already widespread, if controversial, opinion: saving our planet depends on managing the environment.

- Although a best seller, *Collapse* was less successful than Diamond's earlier work *Guns, Germs, and Steel*—possibly because he was attempting to incorporate too much, resulting in a longer, less readable book.

Assessing the Argument

In *Collapse: How Societies Choose to Fail or Survive*, Jared M. Diamond achieved his stated aim. He established a general theory of societal collapse on the basis of comparisons between numerous case studies of both past and present societies, concluding that five key factors cause the fall of these societies. But although his argument is solid and well demonstrated, it did not necessarily challenge previous understandings of societal collapse.

Listing the five key collapse factors, Diamond merely reorganizes and confirms previous conclusions, expanding them on the basis of a broader comparison of cases. Similarly, it is also apparent that the crucial collapse factor—a society's capacity to take corrective action—may be considered self-evident, even if the point had a considerable impact on the environmental debate.[1]

> **❝** If I had the power and means to change only one
> thing of the world today, that one thing would be my
> being limited to change only one thing in the world
> today: my one change would be to give myself the
> power to make many changes. That's because, as I
> discuss in the last chapter of *Collapse*, we face a dozen
> different major problems, all of which we must succeed
> in solving, and any one of which alone could do us in
> even if we solved the other eleven. **❞**
>
> Penguin Reader's Guide, "A Conversation with Jared Diamond"

It follows that Diamond strongly emphasizes the environment as the main cause of societal collapse (while acknowledging other factors such as relations with neighboring groups). Yet, equally, a society's ability to respond to its decline depends above all on its values—its culture, in other words. Diamond insists that this is the most important factor likely to save a society from collapse. Thus it appears that Diamond places equal importance on environment and culture alike.

Achievement in Context

In writing *Collapse*, Diamond did not draw heavily on firsthand ("primary") research. For the most part, he includes personal experiences only in order to provide readers with informal anecdotes that make his analysis more accessible. His fundamental argument is mainly supported by previous historical, anthropological,* archaeological,* and environmental studies, which Diamond distills to form a self-contained answer to his question.

In so doing, he undeniably performs an important service to the study of societal collapse. Indeed, he demonstrates that identifying threads that could be interwoven from so many diverse studies is anything but simple.

The current importance of the environmental debate and the political implications of Diamond's conclusions can also explain the success of his book. He argues that the crucial factor in a societal collapse is the ability of a society, especially of its leaders, to reverse decline. Exactly as was the case in Tikopia in the Pacific, in Japan of the Tokugawa* period (1603–1868), or in the modern Dominican Republic, contemporary leaders can change the destiny of their societies by imposing certain policies.

The wide success of *Collapse* is also due to Diamond's second book, *Guns, Germs, and Steel*,[2] which was awarded several prizes, translated into 25 languages, and sold more than a million copies. People who loved the book's sweeping comparisons about cultures were eager to read another mammoth synthesis of the world's failures and successes—as indeed were those who disagreed with it.

However, like *Guns, Germs, and Steel*, *Collapse* was much more widely appreciated by the general public than by specialists. The latter claimed that the book was flawed, biased, and plainly wrong in many aspects. In contrast, the general public was not necessarily interested in the ideology behind the book or what were asserted to be its scholarly imprecisions. Rather, what non-specialists found valuable was a clear and well-argued case for a conclusion in support of an already widespread opinion: if we want to save our planet, we have to take wise steps to manage the environment. That, perhaps, is the most important achievement of *Collapse*.

Limitations

Diamond argued that the fifth factor—a society's ability to take corrective actions to stave off its own collapse—is the most important factor in a society's survival, this being the single factor that he identified in all the analyzed cases of societal collapse. That said, Diamond does not really explain what this factor comprises.

It is clear that, according to Diamond, the fifteenth-century Norse settlers of Greenland collapsed because they were unable to change their values and learn from the indigenous Inuit people how to cope better with their environment. Similarly, it seems logical that Easter Islanders should have initiated a cultural change at some point between the fifteenth and the seventeenth centuries so as not to cut down their entire forests for the purposes of transporting statues and making canoes. Diamond does not, however, explain what it means to change a culture.

Diamond is much more effective when he describes societies that avoided their collapse; for instance, thanks to the imposition of policies of tree management on the part of the Japanese shoguns or bottom-up micromanagement of horticultural gardens in the Highlands of Papua New Guinea. In other words, it is not difficult to imagine these individual decisions implemented for a higher benefit. What is not clear, however, is how these individual decisions can be considered as an expression of the culture of a people, rather than a set of decisions dictated by the emerging circumstances.

On the basis of the kind of sweeping comparisons upon which so much of Diamond's work is based, it might be possible to isolate a definition of culture as a system of values that can be modified depending on the circumstances. And indeed Diamond does imply, if nothing more, such a concept on the basis of his cross-cultural comparisons. Nonetheless, it remains the case that, while culture occupies the central role in Diamond's theory, it is a concept only partially defined in *Collapse*.

NOTES

1   William Rees, "Contemplating the Abyss," *Nature* 433, no. 7021 (2005): 15–16.

2   Donald Kennedy, "The Choice: Finding Hope in the History of Environmental Ruin," *Foreign Affairs* 84, no. 2 (2005): 134.

MODULE 8
PLACE IN THE AUTHOR'S WORK

KEY POINTS

- Diamond published *Collapse* after achieving worldwide renown with his work *Guns, Germs, and Steel*. Unsurprisingly, the two books have much in common, including style, methodology, and the main question of their research.

- *Collapse* is an integration of many aspects of Diamond's life, including his career, his personal experiences, and his relationships with his public, his coworkers, his friends, and even his enemies.

- While *Collapse* is not the most successful of Jared Diamond's books, it illustrates his life journey as a scholar who began with hard sciences* and then turned to social sciences and popular science writing.

Positioning

Jared M. Diamond was already a world-famous scholar when *Collapse: How Societies Choose to Fail or Survive* was published in 2005. He had come to the attention of the general public with *The Third Chimpanzee*,[1] which won the 1992 Rhône-Poulenc Prize for Science Books and the *Los Angeles Times* Book Prize.

His second book, *Guns, Germs, and Steel*,[2] received worldwide acclaim and several awards, including the Pulitzer Prize in 1998, an Aventis Prize for Science Books, and the 1997 Phi Beta Kappa Award in Science. It was in 1997 that his career really reached a peak. The popular *Why Is Sex Fun?* was also published in that year.

Later, Diamond spent more than five years researching and analyzing the material to write *Collapse*. He was already experienced

> **❝** Diamond is probably the best-known writer of anthropology even though he is not an anthropologist! **❞**
>
> Patricia A. McAnany and Norman Yoffee, *Questioning Collapse*

in drawing together, for the purposes of comparison, substantial quantities of material, covering the entire globe and time spans as long as 13,000 years.

In *Guns, Germs, and Steel,* he used the comparative method* to ask and answer the question of why Europeans were able to dominate the indigenous peoples of Australia, Africa, and the Americas rather than the other way around. His response was a list of environmental causes followed by a series of feedback loops (self-perpetuating cycles of improvements). With *Collapse,* he used the same comparative method, this time to answer another, if related, question: why do societies collapse? The answer, again, is a list of environmental factors that caused some societies to be more favored and others to be less favored.

Although Diamond did not conceive of *Collapse* as a companion to *Guns, Germs, and Steel,* there is a clear intellectual connection between the two books.

Integration

Diamond's intellectual life has had an undeniable influence on his publications. When he was a young PhD student in the field of physiology,* he began by publishing in the specialist field of gall bladder studies. Later, he tried to communicate his interests in physiology with a book unashamedly aimed at general readers, *The Third Chimpanzee.*

At the same time, thanks to his parallel interest in ornithology,* he was increasingly comparing different populations of birds. In the 1990s, working on *Guns, Germs, and Steel,* he combined his ability to write for the general public, his interest in the comparative method, and his recent fascination with human history. The result was his coronation as one of the most important scientists of the decade.

The reaction of the academic world to *Guns, Germs, and Steel* was not, however, always positive. Diamond took academic criticism very seriously; in *Collapse* he made an explicit attempt to avoid charges of ethnocentrism* (tending to adopt one's own cultural theories and values to examine and evaluate other peoples' cultures), social Darwinism* (the discredited idea that individuals and societies are subject to the same evolutionary pressures as biological species), and environmental determinism* (the theory that the environment determines the historical paths of a society associated with a particular territory).

For example, he praises non-Western societies such as the shoguns of Tokugawa-era* Japan, the Polynesians of Tikopia, and the Highlanders of Papua New Guinea for their skillful management of their environmental resources. That seems to have been done in order to avoid charges of ethnocentrism. To take another example, the first chapter of *Collapse* looks more like an ethnography*—a study of the customs, habits, and beliefs of a people—rather than a sweeping comparison.

The book, as a result, includes more ethnography, technical passages, and specific references to academic debates than *Guns, Germs, and Steel*. Diamond also alludes to his anti-racism more frequently in *Collapse* than in *Guns, Germs, and Steel*, as if repetition could clarify a point that he thought he had made already. All this seems to be done to avoid the attacks of his critics.

Significance

Although *Collapse* is not the most successful of Diamond's books, it illustrates his journey as a scholar who began in the so-called hard sciences before turning to social sciences to address what he considered critical questions concerning humanity. To this end, he adopted an approach he called "comparative environmental history"* (a term he uses to describe the study of human societies by comparing in-depth case studies in order to isolate key variables that provide general explanations), writing plain and accessible English to reach the widest possible public.

While Diamond received public acclaim as a result, he was widely attacked by specialists. That had the effect of balancing his intellectual wit with a dose of theoretical humility.[3] In turn, he showed social scientists the power of using "comparative environmental history" in a radically critical way.

Despite the fact that both sides of the controversy appear to have gained something, this does not mean that the debate between Diamond and his academic critics has been resolved. Diamond is constantly charged with being a defender of earlier Western imperialism* and a champion of geographic determinism.

Paradoxically, *Collapse* and *Guns, Germs, and Steel* make plain that, for Diamond, the successes and failures of civilizations do not depend on racial superiority. Rather, in Diamond's view, societies are more or less inclined to develop and collapse as a result of their environmental circumstances. At the same time, collapse and recovery are also the result of other factors, including chance, which demonstrate the multicausative* nature of Diamond's theory as opposed to the determinist position his critics attribute to him ("multicausative" indicates, simply, that a fact results from many causes). Whatever the criticisms of him, then, both books make robust cases.

The significance of Diamond's work is also his message that history and science are not necessarily specialist fields for an intellectual elite. When he explains how he conceived of *Collapse*, it would seem as though anyone sufficiently interested and disciplined might have written it: "It's simple. It was the most fascinating as well as the most important subject I could think of, and one that I'd been interested in for decades, just as many people develop a romantic interest in sites of collapsed societies, like the Maya cities overgrown by jungle or the Anasazi* skyscrapers in the US desert. So there was this romantic mystery that drew me to it."[4]

It follows that one merit of *Collapse* is in making the public feel that science and history can be fun; as such it provides an accessible way to make up your mind on some deeply fascinating questions about humankind.

NOTES

1   Jared M. Diamond, *The Third Chimpanzee: The Evolution and Future of the Human Animal* (London: HarperCollins, 2006).

2   Jared M. Diamond, *Guns, Germs, and Steel* (London: Random House, 2013).

3   See, for example: John R. McNeill, "A Usable Past," *American Scientist* 93, no. 2 (2005): 172–5.

4   Amos Esty, "An Interview with Jared Diamond," *American Scientist Online*, n.d., accessed September 30, 2015, www.americanscientist.org/bookshelf/pub/jared-diamond.

SECTION 3
IMPACT

MODULE 9
THE FIRST RESPONSES

KEY POINTS

- *Collapse* was praised for making a firm point, accessible to a wide audience, in the environmental debate. But it was also severely criticized for the methodology and its alleged ideological premises.

- Although in *Collapse* Diamond had already written "preventive responses" to his critics, the book received those anticipated critiques anyway. Diamond published his responses in relevant journals.

- Sometimes the debate has taken a bitter tone—perhaps on account of what the book represents, politically, ideologically, and morally, in the eyes of the critics, rather than what it says.

Criticism

Jared M. Diamond's *Collapse: How Societies Choose to Fail or Survive* became a best seller in the United States a few days after its publication, perhaps in the wake of the success of *Guns, Germs, and Steel*.[1] It received widespread praise in important newspapers and magazines around the world. In general, favorable reviewers of *Collapse* welcomed the argument advanced by Diamond and its practical impact on society.

For example, William Rees,* a scholar of climate* and sustainable development, noted that *Collapse* makes a firm point in an environmental debate dominated by uncertainty and lack of consensus.[2] Rees praises Diamond for demonstrating that, throughout human history, the crucial variable in the environmental destiny of societies has been the responsibility of people and particularly of their leaders.

> ❝ [T]he notion that the great architectural achievements of the Chaco Canyon can be labeled a societal failure constitutes an example of 'reverse engineering,' meaning the assignation of past failure to contemporary people who have been economically and politically disenfranchised as a direct result of colonial expansion and a European-derived population. ❞
>
> Michael Wilcox, *Questioning Collapse*

Diamond has also been praised for his ability to engage readers from different disciplines or who don't have previous knowledge in any of the specific subjects.[3] In fact, even his critics admit that academic specialization "creates distance from interested laypersons and inquisitive students."[4]

Critics, however, attacked *Collapse* both for the methodology used to support the argument and for its alleged ideological starting points. It is possible to classify these negative reactions into four major themes.

First, critics argued that *Collapse* "represents the persistence of an environmental determinist logic ... referred to as neo-environmental determinism."*[5] That is, they insist that Diamond explains the successes and failures of human societies as mere products of environmental conditions.

Second, critics insisted that Diamond's environmental determinism justifies Western imperialism* (roughly, the ideology justifying the rule of European powers over large territories in Africa, Oceania, and the Americas). The anthropologist Frederick K. Errington* aptly summarized the point: "The haves prosper because of happenstance beyond their control, while the have-nots are responsible for their own demise."[6]

Third, by failing to recognize that no society disappears entirely, this would appear to compromise the validity of the term "collapse"; it is possible, for example, to identify descendants of the Maya, the Indians of the American Southwest, and so on. This point has been particularly stressed by the contributors to the volume *Questioning Collapse*, a work published with the explicit aim of criticizing Diamond's book.[7]

Fourth, Diamond has been accused of ignoring some facts. For example, the archaeologist and anthropologist Terry Hunt* and the archaeologist Carl Lipo* argued that the deforestation* of Easter Island was caused by predatory Polynesian rats, not by the islanders, whose population remained stable until the Europeans brought diseases and slavery[8]—a thesis also put forward by the anthropologist Benny Peiser.*[9]

Responses

In a sense, there was no need to answer the charge of environmental determinism. In *Collapse*, Diamond had already made clear that his argument was not simply a matter of determinism but depended on many explanations; as one scholar has put it, "environmental deterioration always operates as a force among other forces."[10] However, Diamond responded to this and other criticisms on multiple occasions.

He asserted that his critics are biased by the implicit assumption that all geographical explanations are necessarily racist. For him, they are still blindly reacting to the racist tendencies in the social sciences of the nineteenth and twentieth centuries.[11]

Concerning the charge of cultural imperialism, Diamond says he does not blame collapsed societies for their own collapses but rather praises those individuals and groups who take corrective action. For example, the case of preventative polices enacted in the Dominican Republic illustrates that "leaders who don't just react passively, who have the courage to anticipate crises or to act early, and who make strong insightful decisions of top-down management really can make a huge difference to their societies."[12]

With regard to the definition of collapse, for Diamond it "makes no sense to redefine as heartwarmingly resilient a society in which everyone ends up dead, or in which most of the population vanishes, or that loses writing, state government and great art for centuries."[13] Diamond thinks that only those who do not have the necessary knowledge of animals, plants, soils, and climates can deny the destruction that results from environmental degradation.*[14]

In terms of the historical facts, Diamond notes that deforestation in Easter Island cannot be attributed to rats, which were present in other Polynesian islands without necessarily causing deforestation. He adds that this and other conclusions by Hunt and Lipo "are considered transparently wrong by essentially all other archaeologists with active programs on Easter Island."[15]

Conflict and Consensus

Whether some consensus is found between Diamond and his critics largely depends on the tone of the debate and the content of the criticism. For example, Diamond writes, "whenever I hear the words 'geographic determinism,' I know that I am about to hear a reflex dismissal of geographic considerations, an opinion not worth listening to or reading, and an excuse for intellectual laziness and for not coming to grips with real issues." In contrast, when a journalist asked Diamond whether any criticism caused him to rethink aspects of the book, he responded, "Details, yes; main thrusts of my argument, no."[16] It follows that some critics were rightly pointing at certain inaccuracies, whereas others have been dismissed for failing to provide evidence to back up their criticisms.

In general, however, the distance between Diamond and his critics means that agreement is always unlikely. Rather, arguments tend to be dismissed on the grounds of incompetence and lack of specialist knowledge. If Diamond says that his critics are not trained geographers,[17] for example, they respond by asserting that he is not a trained historian.[18] It is not always productive.

The fact that neither side is able to engage on equal terms is not to be understood as a consequence of what Diamond actually says in *Collapse*, which is mostly a synthesis of arguments advanced by previous scholars. Rather, the reasons behind the vitriolic tone of Diamond's critics stem more from what they hold the book to represent politically, ideologically, and morally—perhaps their true objection.

NOTES

1 Donald Kennedy, "The Choice: Finding Hope in the History of Environmental Ruin," *Foreign Affairs* 84, no. 2 (2005): 134–8.

2 William Rees, "Contemplating the Abyss," *Nature* 433, no. 7021 (January 6, 2005): 15–16.

3 John R. McNeill, "A Usable Past," *American Scientist* 93, no. 2 (March 1, 2005): 174.

4 Patricia A. McAnany and Norman Yoffee, eds., *Questioning Collapse: Human Resilience, Ecological Vulnerability, and the Aftermath of Empire* (New York, NY: Cambridge University Press, 2010), 4.

5 Gabriel Judkins et al., "Determinism within Human–Environment Research and the Rediscovery of Environmental Causation," *The Geographical Journal* 174, no. 1 (2008): 18.

6 George Johnson, "A Question of Blame When Societies Fall," *The New York Times*, December 25, 2007, accessed September 30, 2015, www.nytimes.com/2007/12/25/science/25diam.html.

7 McAnany and Yoffee, *Questioning Collapse.*

8 Terry Hunt and Carl Lipo, "Ecological Catastrophe, Collapse, and the Myth of 'Ecocide' on Rapa Nui (Easter Island)," in *Questioning Collapse,* McAnany and Yoffee, 223–46.

9 Benny Peiser, "From Genocide to Ecocide: The Rape of Rapa Nui," *Energy & Environment* 16, no. 3 (2005): 513–40.

10 McNeill, "A Usable Past," 172.

11 Jared M. Diamond, "Geographic Determinism: What Does 'Geographic Determinism' Really Mean?," jareddiamond.org, n.d., accessed September 30, 2015, www.jareddiamond.org/Jared_Diamond/Geographic_determinism.html.

12 Jared M. Diamond, *Collapse: How Societies Choose to Fail or Survive* (London: Penguin, 2011), 304.

13 Jared M. Diamond, "Two Views of Collapse," *Nature* 463, no. 7283 (2010): 881.

14 Diamond, "Geographic Determinism."

15 Mark Lynas, "The Myths of Easter Island—Jared Diamond Responds," marklynas.org, September 22, 2011, accessed September 10, 2015, www.marklynas.org/2011/09/the-myths-of-easter-island-jared-diamond-responds/.

16 Penguin Reader's Guide, "A Conversation with Jared Diamond," penguin.com, n.d., accessed September 9, 2015, www.penguin.com/read/book-clubs/collapse/9780143117001.

17 Diamond, "Geographic Determinism."

18 Anthony J. McMichael, "Collapse. How Societies Choose to Fail or Succeed. Jared Diamond," *International Journal of Epidemiology* 35, no. 2 (April 1, 2006): 499–500.

MODULE 10
THE EVOLVING DEBATE

KEY POINTS

- It could be argued that in the academic debate about indigenous rights and Western imperialism,* Diamond's arguments have been misrepresented.

- Much of the debate between Diamond and his opponents has been dominated by the projection of different approaches to knowledge concerning the degree to which comparisons are useful or possible.

- In current scholarship, debates about factual evidence and methodology tend simply to stall in the face of an apparently implacable hostility between Diamond and many anthropologists.

Uses and Problems

In an academic context, the problem with using the theory proposed by Jared M. Diamond's *Collapse: How Societies Choose to Fail or Survive* is that the debate over its value is not necessarily about what the work argues but, rather, about what its critics claim it argues. For example, in the article "F**k Jared Diamond," the American scholar and activist David Correia* writes, "Everything Diamond does is motivated by an environmental determinism* that takes the physical environment, including the climate,* to be a determinant on human society."[1] As Diamond explains, however, "in the strict sense [environmental determinism] is not a view that any sensible person espouses today. Instead, historians who discuss environmental influences on history at all are often caricatured by critics as 'environmental determinists,' supposedly meaning someone who believes that the environment strictly determines human history and that human choices count for

> ❝ In offering this framework, Diamond goes beyond simplistic formulations about ecological collapse, recognizing that environmental deterioration always operates as a force among other forces, and sometimes in synergistic conjunction with other forces. ❞
>
> John R. McNeill, "A Usable Past"

nothing."[2] It seems that *Collapse*, like *Guns, Germs, and Steel*, is held to be a product of this old school of environmental determinist thought without the book necessarily espousing this school's tenets.

Hence, the charge of determinism is not necessarily associated with the book's argument. Instead, the ferocity of the debate is perhaps better explained by preexisting tensions between Diamond and his critics. For example, some anthropologists have criticized Diamond because his theory allegedly supports the "ideology of an imperial capitalism," as the geographer Dick Peet called it[3] (capitalism being the economic and social system, dominant in the West today, in which trade and industry are held in private hands). In contrast, some anthropologists see themselves as defenders of indigenous rights against what they consider the homogenizing forces of globalization* (the convergence of political, economic, and cultural ties and habits across continents) and the socioeconomic inequalities introduced by Western capitalism.[4] Neither view is necessarily valid, for Diamond never explicitly justified Western imperialism, and no indigenous people see themselves as requiring the kind of protection that some anthropologists extend to them. But there is a case to be made that in the course of the debate, Diamond has been attacked for views he does not hold.

Schools of Thought

Another interpretation concerns the ways in which *Collapse* was used in the debate about the opposition between nomothetic* and

65

ideographic approaches.* "Nomothetic" describes the possibility of deriving general ideas or laws from a set of particular facts; "ideographic," by contrast, describes the assumption that no phenomena are truly comparable, and only concrete properties are worthy of description.

Although an argument of very long standing, the fact that the controversy was still alive at the time when Diamond was forming his ideas is evidenced by a debate in 1988 at the University of Manchester; on that occasion, 37 anthropologists voted against the motion that their discipline was a generalizing science while 26 agreed with it.

Almost three decades later, the anthropologist Alex Golub* wrote that "the one lesson [American] anthropologists want to spread across the world is 'It's complicated.' In classrooms and publications, our goal is to show the complexity of human life to our audiences. To the horror of nomothetic, model-making sciences, for us 'abstraction' and 'simplification' are often pejorative terms."[5] This shows that the opposition is still alive today.

In *Collapse*, Diamond's intention was not necessarily to persuade his critics that cross-cultural comparison and the natural experiment* are infallible scientific methods. However, the skepticism with which anthropologists read *Collapse* relates to a more general dissatisfaction with all-encompassing arguments about human societies as opposed to those emphasizing complexity.

This emphasis on complexity dates back at least to the days of the pioneering anthropologist Franz Boas,* who strongly rejected the possibility of establishing general theories about all human societies. He insisted that the goal of anthropology was ethnographic* description, based on what he called "historical particularism" (roughly, the idea that any society is the product of its unique historical circumstances). Other anthropologists have nevertheless attempted to establish general theories. For example, it is on the basis of cross-cultural comparisons that in 1925 the influential French sociologist Marcel Mauss* wrote *The Gift*, perhaps the most popular book in anthropology.

It follows that the opposition between nomothetic and idiographic approaches is inherent to anthropology itself rather than one which sets up anthropologists in opposition to Diamond.

In Current Scholarship

Arguably, the widespread popularity and success of Diamond's work has, to specialists, been detrimental to the diffusion of the points he has made. Indeed, his arguments have repeatedly been appropriated and misrepresented. It is a distortion of his views common to both the academic and the wider world.

In a speech in Jerusalem in 2012, the conservative US politician Mitt Romney* referred to Diamond's work to support his view that the differences between Israel and Palestine in terms of industrial development could be explained as the consequences of cultural differences. That was fundamental to his contention that conservative American culture is the single most critical reason for the material and military success of the United States. Diamond responded in a *New York Times* article explaining that Romney had misunderstood his argument.[6]

In the academic context, Diamond believes that criticisms of his book are not based on the evidence he assembles but on moral grounds. For example, he thinks the authors of the critical book *Questioning Collapse* "query the interpretation of past societal demises, preferring a positive message about human nature."[7] They "dismiss as an 'accident of geography' those explanations ... that rest on environmental factors—such as continental differences in biogeographic endowments,* shapes and locations—but they do not offer a substitute thesis."[8] ("Biogeographic endowments" refers to the distribution of species of plants and animals in a certain area at a specific time.)

While Diamond acknowledges that some societies are resilient enough to survive even extreme crises (an idea strongly advanced in

Questioning Collapse), he criticizes the authors for illustrating it inappropriately. "For instance, one chapter claims that the Greenland Norse people emigrated rather than dying out, despite no evidence for that claim and despite graphic archaeological evidence of starvation—bones and debris in the topmost archaeological layer from the final winter of the Greenland Western Settlement's existence."[9]

It is rare that any resolution is found in this kind of debate about factual evidence and methodology; the discipline of anthropology has, meanwhile, earned a reputation for uniquely berating Diamond.[10]

NOTES

1 David Correia, "F**k Jared Diamond," *Capitalism Nature Socialism* 24, no. 4 (2013): 1–6.

2 Penguin Reader's Guide, "A Conversation with Jared Diamond," penguin. com, n.d., accessed September 9, 2015, www.penguin.com/read/book-clubs/collapse/9780143117001.

3 Correia, "F**k Jared Diamond," 4.

4 See, for example: Tony Crook, "Indigenous Human Rights," *Anthropology Today* 14, no. 1 (1998): 18–19.

5 Alex Golub, "Game of Thrones and Anthropology," *Savage Minds*, July 2, 2014, accessed September 10, 2015, http://savageminds. org/2014/07/02/game-of-thrones-and-anthropology/.

6 Jared M. Diamond, "Romney Hasn't Done His Homework," *The New York Times,* August 1, 2012, accessed September 30, 2015, www.nytimes. com/2012/08/02/opinion/mitt-romneys-search-for-simple-answers.html.

7 Jared M. Diamond, "Two Views of Collapse," *Nature* 463, no. 7283 (February 18, 2010): 880.

8 Diamond, "Two Views of Collapse," 880.

9 Diamond, "Two Views of Collapse," 880.

10 Jason Antrosio, "Jared Diamond and Future Public Anthropology," livinganthropologically.com, July 21, 2014, accessed September 10, 2015, www.livinganthropologically.com/2014/07/21/jared-diamond-future-public-anthropology/.

MODULE 11
IMPACT AND INFLUENCE TODAY

KEY POINTS

- *Collapse* is an important work for anyone interested in grand narratives of human history. But readers must be aware of the fierce debate that the book has sparked.

- *Collapse* is cited in discussions in many disciplines, including anthropology,* archaeology,* history, and geography. But it has rarely served to clinch any dispute.

- The only point on which all scholars agree is the popularity of *Collapse* among the general public—the result of Diamond's talent for popularizing science. Its influence remains uncontested.

Position

Jared M. Diamond's *Collapse: How Societies Choose to Fail or Survive* may well be a book with wide appeal for anyone interested in great historical sweeps. But readers must be aware of the heated debate that it, and similar works by Diamond, have provoked. Depending on one's take on them, the arguments advanced in *Collapse* can be understood in different ways: from the factually valid to lacking evidence; from the methodologically solid to the theoretically unsustainable; from the politically correct to the morally unacceptable. In particular, the moral and political positions attributed to *Collapse* remain controversial.

One widespread reading of *Collapse* among social scientists is that "Diamond's narrative of disappearance and marginalization is one of conquest's most potent instruments."[1] Also, "Collapse focuses on cases of indigenous environmental mismanagement, suggesting that the world's 'have nots' often wound up that way because they 'chose' to overshoot their environmental limitations and their societies fell apart as a result."[2]

> **❝** … a complete roster of potentially relevant variables leads to an unworkably complex model, and Diamond has the virtue of simplicity. **❞**
>
> John R. McNeill, "A Usable Past"

Diamond was explicit in not supporting such a moral or political position. He declared that he wrote *Guns, Germs, and Steel* in order to convince Westerners that European domination is not the result of racial superiority. He wanted to show that Western prosperity depends on factors that have always been at least partly beyond will or merit.

Again, in *Collapse* he maintained this emphasis on environmental factors as a way to demonstrate that any racial explanation is unsubstantial. But he also highlighted the importance of individual action as a way to place more responsibility on actual human beings (as was the case in, for example, the Dominican Republic, where preventative environmental policies were enacted by the dictators Rafael Trujillo* and Joaquin Balaguer*).

Praising the environmentally friendly policies of dictators was not a happy choice. But the morality of the Dominican Republic's repressive rulers is not relevant in the discussion about the environmental impact of their policies. What matters is rather that individual choices made a difference to the fate of a society, regardless of whose actions they were.

Interaction

Collapse, like other works by Diamond, has a bearing on debates concerning a number of disciplines, notably anthropology, archaeology, history, and geography. But these debates do not necessarily end with agreement and eventually run out of energy thanks to the absolute disagreement between Diamond and his critics.

The discussion concerning the factual evidence behind the arguments advanced in *Collapse* has slowly faded, for example, with neither side able to demonstrate that its historical understanding and its use of evidence is superior to the other's. The contributors to the volume *Questioning Collapse* contend that there was never a forest in the Chaco Canyon in New Mexico and that consequently the native Anasazi* could not have deforested what never existed. They further argue that analysis of plant remains in ancient pack-rat middens* (piles of refuse assembled by rodents) there "reveal a climate* and ecology* almost exactly like that which exists today."[3] Diamond, on the other hand, has insisted that "radiocarbon dating of middens revealed a former pinyon-juniper woodland that is now absent from the canyon."[4] Hence, both Diamond and his critics put forward arguments and evidence to support them that remain incompatible. Given this, the debate, confronted by these irreconcilable positions, has tended to stagnate.

The argument concerning environmental determinism* has also come to a halt for precisely the lack of any common ground. For example, historians blame Diamond for not giving enough weight to the role of contingency based on individual decisions and chance. Contrarily, he blames them for denying the role of environmental causes in cultural traits.[5]

While these debates are mostly relevant for an arena of specialists, *Collapse* has also had an undeniable influence on public discussions. Unconcerned by specialist debates, readers have become increasingly interested in such themes as climate change,* environmental damage, cultural relativism (the belief that it is vital to take an individual's culture into account when interpreting his or her actions), and the possibility of learning from the different fates of human societies.[6]

Although these are merits, it can also be argued that Diamond has invited much skepticism from specialists precisely because he insisted on writing for a non-specialist audience.

The Continuing Debate

The debate about *Collapse* and other works by Diamond is ongoing, even if the focus changes constantly. Some critics hone in more on the material in support of Diamond's theory, some on the moral and political implications of the book, some on its theoretical value. But most of these debates tend to stall in the absence of any lack of conclusive evidence to support either side, arguably because the substantial basis of the debate is flawed. While Diamond is caricatured by his critics, it has been argued that his critics, too, "get caricatured by being slotted into one of many already-rehearsed 'you're just' tropes:

- You're just angry because Diamond isn't an anthropologist.
- You're just jealous because Diamond is popular.
- You're just a nitpicking specialist—Diamond is a big-ideas man.
- You're just playing by academic rules—Diamond is an intellectual.
- You're just calling Diamond a determinist, and he isn't a determinist."[7]

Whether as a result of professional envy, charges of oversimplification, lack of further factual evidence, intellectual preferences, or disputed theoretical positions, the debates remain unresolved.

Nevertheless: scholars agree that *Collapse,* as much as other works by Diamond, has had a strong impact on society. This depends primarily on Diamond's writing style, which, as even his critics recognize, engages readers who are otherwise distant from scientific issues. Prompted by Diamond's readability and accessibility, some anthropologists have also made "an effort to shorten that distance,"[8] presumably by making their writing more accessible.

NOTES

1   Michael Wilcox, "Marketing Conquest and the Vanishing Indian: An Indigenous Response to Jared Diamond's Archaeology of the American Southwest," in *Questioning Collapse: Human Resilience, Ecological Vulnerability, and the Aftermath of Empire*, ed. Patricia A. McAnany and Norman Yoffee (New York, NY: Cambridge University Press, 2010), 138.

2   James L. Flexner, "Questioning Collapse: Human Resilience, Ecological Vulnerability, and the Aftermath of Empire," *Pacific Affairs* 84, no. 4 (2011), 741.

3   Jared M. Diamond, "Two Views of Collapse," *Nature* 463, no. 7283 (2010): 880–1.

4   Diamond, "Two Views of Collapse," 881.

5   Jared M. Diamond, "Geographic Determinism: What Does 'Geographic Determinism' Really Mean?," jareddiamond.org, n.d., accessed September 30, 2015, www.jareddiamond.org/Jared_Diamond/Geographic_determinism.html.

6   Mark Lynas, "The Myths of Easter Island—Jared Diamond Responds," marklynas.org, September 22, 2011, accessed September 10, 2015, www.marklynas.org/2011/09/the-myths-of-easter-island-jared-diamond-responds/.

7   Jason Antrosio, "Jared Diamond Won't Beat Mitt Romney – Anthropolitics 2012," livinganthropologically.com, August 4, 2012, accessed September 10, 2015, www.livinganthropologically.com/2012/08/04/diamond-romney/.

8   McAnany and Yoffee, *Questioning Collapse*. See also: Jeremy MacClancy and Chris McDonaugh, eds., *Popularizing Anthropology* (London: Routledge, 2002).

MODULE 12
WHERE NEXT?

KEY POINTS

- Jared Diamond's *Collapse*, a book about societies in many different parts of the world in many different periods, was successful across the globe. Anthropologists* are increasingly anxious to have such an impact themselves. They can no longer ignore or dismiss the fact that such complex questions have been successfully popularized.

- It is unlikely that other scholars will imitate Diamond's intellectual style; most academics still value complexity above accessibility (which might explain why they seldom reach wider audiences).

- *Collapse* advances an argument that concerns humanity as a whole. Grand theories of this kind appeal on a popular level but encounter the skepticism of specialists.

Potential

Collapse: How Societies Choose to Fail or Survive by Jared M. Diamond is a global best seller written by a Pulitzer Prize-winning author, translated into dozens of languages. It has even been turned into a documentary produced in the United States by the National Geographic Society.* A revised edition with an additional chapter on the Cambodian region of Angkor* was published in 2011.

It has undeniably left a mark on both the study of societal collapse and on the public debate about climate change* and environmental damage. It is likely to maintain its position and, potentially, influence future scholarship and public discussion, especially because it makes plain the reach of Diamond's approach to big questions for humanity.

> ❝Yes, there is something next, another big book about another big question of human history and human societies. I hope to complete that new book in about another five years. But, as Conan Doyle let Sherlock Holmes explain to Dr. Watson in alluding to the mystery of the giant rat of Sumatra, 'The world is not yet ready for this story.'❞
>
> Penguin Reader's Guide, "A Conversation with Jared Diamond"

What *Collapse* presents, however, is not necessarily new data or methodology. Rather, *Collapse* expands the synthesis of preexisting case studies to the point of offering an unparalleled span of human history, and advances a theoretical argument about the entirety of humankind. It is an example of its author's successful formula: a clear question relevant for humanity as a whole, the comparative method,* and the offer of a succinct answer. Ultimately, it is the popularity of this formula that will grant the text continuing relevance, even though it will also be associated with the many controversies it spurred.

As Diamond's formula has ensured widespread and long-standing success for his books, we might predict that the formula will be applied to future works in pursuit of similar outcomes. In the context of anthropology, to take the example of one discipline among many, scholars have already started to reflect on what they can learn from Diamond to make their own books more widely read and relevant in the public spheres.

For example, in a panel organized at the 2013 meetings of the American Anthropological Association, anthropologists discussed the accessibility of Diamond's work to laypersons, and its resulting relevance for the public debate. This fact suggests that something is changing. Anthropologists increasingly recognize that, although they "shudder at Jared-Diamond-as-Anthropology, it is pretty much standard for how the undergraduate-level audience gets their anthropology and world history."[1] It is undeniable that Diamond's work is now "a primary conduit for how people think they know what they know about culture and cultural relativism"[2] (the belief that, when interpreting an individual's actions and belief, we must take the context of his or her culture into account). For this reason, they think that the "tactic of ignoring Diamond—or ... the structures that make a Jared Diamond possible—cannot be sustained."[3]

Future Directions

Collapse is an example of Diamond's formula for making academic subjects more accessible to a wider public. Scholars of the humanities and social sciences interested in having an impact on society might want to look at it as a model. Social scientists are increasingly aware of the relevance of this approach, with the Research Excellence Framework, a body that assesses the quality of research in the United Kingdom, considering the impact on "economy, society, public policy, culture and the quality of life" as the main criteria of evaluation.

Even though *Collapse* illustrates one way in which social sciences can be made more relevant in the public debate, however, it is unlikely that other scholars will imitate Diamond's intellectual style. Social scientists tend to oppose authors who draw conclusions on the basis of broad comparisons. That is particularly true of anthropologists, who reject the possibility of simple answers and emphasize the complexity of sociocultural realities.[4]

Nevertheless, "In contemporary anthropology, pleas for narrative have almost become a cliché ... but we rarely get on with actually telling stories. Maybe this is general professional affliction,"[5] wrote the anthropologist Thomas Hylland Eriksen.* In contrast, "Diamond has a gift for storytelling."[6] Anthropologists recognize that it is an ancient and distinctly human desire to tell a story and to tell it well.[7] But notwithstanding these authors' efforts at solving the apparent incompatibility between complexity and narrative, no anthropologist has yet achieved the widespread popularity of Diamond.

Summary

A best seller within days of its publication, *Collapse* was subsequently made into a documentary and provoked debate inside and outside of academia; while its argument, methodology, and theoretical reach—not to mention its political and moral stand—have been questioned, its popular success remains unchallenged.

Indeed, it is precisely its popularity beyond the academic world that has generated so much criticism among specialists. *Collapse* advances an argument about the fate of human societies that concerns humanity in its totality. Grand theories of this kind appeal to the public but rarely win over skeptical specialists.

Another explanation for its popularity outside of academia is Diamond's use of the comparative method. Whatever its appeal to non-specialists, many contemporary scholars see such a method as inappropriate because it overestimates similarities and underestimates differences.

Finally, however, whether you agree with Diamond or not, the impact of his books remains beyond dispute.

NOTES

1   Jason Antrosio, "Jared Diamond and Future Public Anthropology," livinganthropologically.com, July 21, 2014, accessed September 10, 2015, www.livinganthropologically.com/2014/07/21/jared-diamond-future-public-anthropology/.

2   Antrosio, "Jared Diamond."

3   Antrosio, "Jared Diamond."

4   Antrosio, "Jared Diamond."

5   Thomas H. Eriksen, *Engaging Anthropology: The Case for a Public Presence* (Oxford, UK; New York, NY: Berg, 2006).

6   Bryn Williams, "Can You Trust Jared Diamond?" *Slate*, February 18, 2013, accessed September 30, 2015, www.slate.com/articles/health_and_ science/books/2013/02/jared_diamond_the_world_until_yesterday_ anthropologists_are_wary_of_lack.html.

7   Patricia A. McAnany and Norman Yoffee, eds., *Questioning Collapse: Human Resilience, Ecological Vulnerability, and the Aftermath of Empire* (New York, NY: Cambridge University Press, 2010), 1.

GLOSSARY

GLOSSARY OF TERMS

Anasazi: a term originating in the Navajo language, indicating the ancient inhabitants of the territory comprising contemporary southern Utah, northern Arizona, northwestern New Mexico, and southwestern Colorado. Current consensus dates their origin to around the twelfth century B.C.E. In *Collapse*, Diamond deals with different Anasazi groups and cultures that collapsed between the twelfth and fifteenth centuries C.E.

Anthropology: the study of humankind. It breaks down into multiple subfields, each focusing on one specific aspect, such as culture, social institutions, language, biology, and economy, among others.

Archaeology: the scientific study of past human activity by means of the examination of ancient bones, artifacts, and environmental modifications.

Axiology: a theory of value—that is, of all things that a particular group of people considers valuable. In the context of the societies studied by Diamond, the values of a society determined a people's ability to overcome societal collapse.

Biodiversity: the measure indicating the number and variety of organisms (both animal and vegetal) in a given ecosystem. It varies across the globe and determines a variety of advantages for local inhabitants. For example, greater biodiversity increases fodder yield, crop yield, and wood production.

Biogeographic endowment: the distribution of species of plants and animals in a geographic space at a particular time.

Biophysics: a discipline that studies biological systems, such as the human body, with methods borrowed from physics.

Botany: the scientific study of plants.

Chiefdoms: an independent political organization in which status is granted as a consequence of belonging to a descent group. Individuals are ranked on the basis of their kinship proximity to a paramount chief.

Climate: the long-term, large-scale pattern of variation in meteorological variables such as temperature, precipitation, wind, and humidity. It differs from weather, which indicates the short-term pattern of variation in meteorological variables in a relatively smaller location.

Climate change: the long-term, large-scale fluctuation in climate: decades of drought, a century of wet weather, or the Little Ice Age of the seventeenth to the nineteenth centuries. Today this term, which Diamond uses consistently throughout *Collapse*, is often taken to mean "catastrophic anthropogenic (human-activated) global warming." Climate change is not exclusively caused by human beings, however, and also occurs thanks to natural causes; moreover, it does not necessarily result in a warmer climate, but one that can be colder, wetter, drier, and more or less variable.

Comparative environmental history: an expression used by Diamond to indicate a method for studying human societies, which consists of comparing in-depth case studies of different societies in order to isolate key variables that provide general explanations.

Comparative method: a method of research and analysis that consists of the examination of two or more cases and identifying similarities and differences that might explain their respective outcomes.

Continental axis: an imaginary line traced horizontally on a continent whose territory extends for longer from east to west than from north to south. Vice versa, the line is traced vertically if the territory of a continent extends for longer from north to south than from east to west.

Cultural imperialism: the imposition by a dominant group of a particular culture upon a dominated group. It can take various forms, ranging from military control to indoctrination.

Cultural possibilism: a theory in geography that says culture is shaped by social rather than environmental conditions. It follows that its approach is directly opposed to geographical determinism.

Deforestation: the removal of trees from a given territory. The main cause of deforestation is agriculture, including subsistence farming, commercial agriculture, and logging.

Ecology: the scientific study of the relations between organisms and their habitat. Ecologists advocate the sustainable management of environmental resources through changes in public policies and individual behavior.

Empiricism: a theory of knowledge that considers direct observation as the sole method of obtaining reliable knowledge.

Environmental degradation: the deterioration of an ecosystem due to the progressive exhaustion of its resources. It results in the depletion of air, water, and soil quality and the extinction of wildlife.

Environmental determinism: a theory suggesting that the environment determines the historical trajectories (paths) of a society associated with a particular territory. Its extreme tenets hold that individual actions cannot substantially alter the influence of environmental factors—such as climate, fauna (animals), flora (plants), and continental axis—on the fate of a society.

Environmental history: the scientific study of the relationship between human societies and their environment through time.

Erosion: the movement of soil and rock from one location to another, caused by such factors as rain, wind, agriculture, and deforestation. One major consequence of erosion is land degradation, which in turn decreases soil fertility.

Ethnocentrism: a tendency to adopt one's own cultural theories and values to examine and evaluate other people's cultures. Generally, ethnocentrism implies that one's own culture is somehow superior to the culture of other people.

Ethnography: the scientific study of groups of people, along with their customs, habits, and beliefs.

Geographic determinism: see Environmental determinism.

Globalization: the process of increasing interconnectedness among the people of the world, characterized by increasingly rapid and frequent travel, communications, and material exchanges.

Hard sciences: a popular expression that is often used to indicate the natural or physical sciences. Disciplines such as chemistry, biology, and physics are considered "hard sciences" by virtue of their usage of hypotheses and experiments as methodologies to understand the universe.

Hypertrophy: a term borrowed from medicine to indicate the excessive growth of a system or structure.

Idiographic approach: the idea that no phenomena can be comparable. It encourages the description of concrete properties, not the abstraction of general ideas or laws.

Immobilism: the inability or unwillingness to take political action, often a result of conservative values.

Independent variable: an expression borrowed from mathematics to indicate the external cause of a phenomenon.

Interdisciplinarity: a combination of different academic disciplines in a single research activity. It differs from multidisciplinarity in that it synthesizes multiple disciplines into a new kind of research activity rather than solving a particular research problem with many separate contributions.

Laboratory conditions: the absence of external interference in a controlled environment in which a phenomenon is scientifically studied.

Little Ice Age: a period of the Earth's climatic history that took place from about 1400 C.E. to 1800 C.E. During this time, the mean temperature in the Northern hemisphere decreased considerably.

Malthusian trap: the theory, proposed by the English economist and demographer Thomas Malthus, that the exponential growth of human populations tends to outrun the arithmetic growth of food production.

Midden: a concentration of ancient waste products left in a particular location. These heaps of remains, excrement, and all sorts of old material are extremely useful for archaeologists who study past societies.

Multicausative: a term indicating a fact that resulted from multiple causes which combined with each other. Diamond's theory, for example, is multicausative because it explains societal collapses as resulting from the combination of five collapse factors.

Multidisciplinarity: an approach that involves contributions from multiple disciplines for the sake of addressing complex problems that one single discipline can only partially help to solve or describe.

National Geographic: the journal of the US National Geographic Society, published continuously since 1888.

Natural experiment: the observation of a context (such as a group of people in a given territory) exposed to influences beyond the control of the investigators, who attempt to establish causal connections between the exposure and the changes in the object of study.

Nomothetic approach: an idea suggesting the possibility of abstracting general ideas or laws from a set of particular facts. The term "nomothetic" is often opposed to idiographic.

Ornithology: the systematic, scientific study of birds.

Per capita income: a measure of the average income earned by a person in a given territory, calculated by dividing the total income in the area by the total population.

Photosynthetic capacity: the amount of sunlight per acre that the Earth is able to absorb. Regardless of the quantity of light produced by the sun, there is a maximum amount that can be absorbed. That means that, if man-made areas absorb most of the sunlight, there is not much sunlight left for natural ecosystems.

Physiology: a subdiscipline of biology that studies the normal functioning of living organisms.

Pollen and charcoal analysis: a method of determining the presence of species of plants in a given territory through the analysis of their remains.

Polymath: a person with a multiplicity of interests and in-depth knowledge in a diversity of disciplines. Often, polymaths combine theoretical and practical knowledge with the ability to speak multiple languages and play numerous instruments.

Postclassic period: a period of Mesoamerican history from about 950 to 1539 C.E.

Pre-Columbian Maya: a Mesoamerican civilization developed before 2000 B.C.E. in the area encompassing southeastern Mexico, Guatemala, Belize, the western part of El Salvador, and Honduras. It collapsed partly because of the drought caused by cutting trees to the point of irreversible deforestation. This altered the local water cycling and decreased rainfalls, resulting in a protracted drought.

Radiocarbon dating: a method that determines the age of an object by measuring the quantity of radiocarbon, a radioactive isotope of carbon, it contains. Since the quantity of radiocarbon in an animal or plant decreases constantly after death, it is possible to calculate approximately when the animal or plant died.

Reforestation: an increase in the number of living trees per acre as a consequence of human intentional plantation or natural growth in a previously deforested area.

Resilience: the ability of a system, such as a society or living organism, to cope with changes and challenges. For example, climate resilience indicates the capacity of an ecological context or human society to adapt to long-term changes in temperature or humidity.

Rwanda: an east-central equatorial African nation; from April to July 1994, it saw the massacre of some 500,000–1,000,000 people, the greatest majority of whom were of the Tutsi ethnic group, at the hands of members of the Hutu ethnic group.

Salinization: an increase in the presence of salt in the soil. The consequences of salinization include reduced plant growth and yield, reduced water quality, and increased soil erosion.

Social Darwinism: a group of theories that explain human phenomena in terms of evolution, natural selection, and survival of the fittest. The expression derives from Charles Darwin's theory of natural selection, which was not initially meant to be applied to sociocultural issues. Critics of racist and imperialist views that nature makes "winners" and "losers" invented this term.

Sustainability: the ability to make use of environmental resources without exhausting them or damaging the environment.

Tokugawa Japan: a period of Japanese history in which Japanese society was ruled by the Tokugawa shogunate, a feudal military government that lasted from 1603 to 1868.

Water management: the ability to use water resources without exhausting them, reducing their qualities, or damaging the environment.

Western imperialism: an expression that roughly indicates the ideology justifying the rule of European powers over large territories in Africa, Oceania, and the Americas. Such justification is often given in racial terms, whereby these continents should not be controlled and governed by their inhabitants, but by those who, by virtue of racial superiority, can do so more efficiently.

PEOPLE MENTIONED IN THE TEXT

Aristotle (384–322 B.C.E.) was a philosopher and scientist at Plato's Academy in ancient Athens, Greece. He explained the cultural differences between Northern Europeans, Asians, and Greeks as caused by different climatic conditions.

Paul Bahn is a British archaeologist, translator, writer, and broadcaster who has published extensively on a range of archaeological topics, including *The Enigmas of Easter Island* (with John Flenley, 2003).

Joaquin Balaguer (1906–2002) was the president of the Dominican Republic for three non-consecutive terms between 1960 and 1996.

Franz Boas (1858–1942) was a Prussian-born anthropologist who has been called the "father of American anthropology." He rejected evolutionary approaches to the study of culture and promoted historical particularism and cultural relativism.

Mark Brenner is a limnologist and paleolimnologist (scholar of bodies of water such as rivers and lakes), with special interests in tropical and subtropical lakes and watersheds. He reconstructs the history of aquatic ecosystems on the basis of sediment cores from the bottoms of lakes.

David Correia (b. 1968) is an American scholar and activist, and an associate professor of American studies at the University of New Mexico.

George Cowgill (b. 1929) is an American anthropologist and archaeologist with fieldwork experience in Teotihuacán, Mexico. He contributed to the comparative study of ancient states and cities with numerous publications.

Jason H. Curtis works as a senior associate in geochemistry at the University of Florida and is an expert in climatic variation in ancient societies.

Thomas Hylland Eriksen (b. 1962) is a Norwegian professor of social anthropology at the University of Oslo and currently president of the European Association of Social Anthropologists. One of his research interests focuses on the popularization of social anthropology.

Frederick K. Errington is emeritus professor of anthropology at Trinity College, with research experience in Papua New Guinea, Sumatra, and Montana. Much of his work is done in collaboration with his wife Deborah Gewertz.

Brian Fagan (b. 1936) is an archaeologist and anthropologist with fieldwork experience in Africa.

John Flenley is emeritus professor in biogeography at Massey University, New Zealand and a palynologist (a specialist in "dust"— pollen and spores). He has published prolifically in the field of paleopalynology.

Alex Golub is an anthropologist with fieldwork experience in Papua New Guinea. He is the founder of the popular cultural anthropology website savageminds.org, which has long engaged with the work of Jared Diamond.

Hippocrates (460–370 B.C.E.) is referred to as the "father of Western medicine." He believed the environment was responsible for major features of human character, body, and culture.

David A. Hodell (b. 1958) is a geologist and paleoclimatologist working as professor of geology at the University of Cambridge. His research with Brenner, Curtis, and Guilderson focused on the collapse of the Maya Empire.

Terry Hunt is an archaeologist and a professor of anthropology at the University of Oregon. His research focuses on environmental change and life on the islands of the Pacific Ocean. He has published extensively in the fields of Pacific archaeology, prehistory, and linguistics.

Carl Lipo is an archaeologist who has done research on prehistoric potters of the Mississippi Valley and the construction of the famous Easter Island's moai.

Marcel Mauss (1872–1950) was a French sociologist, although he is best known for his anthropological book *The Gift* (1925), which compares the circulation of objects in different past and present societies.

Patricia A. McAnany (b.1953) is a Kenan eminent professor of anthropology, University of North Carolina, who conducted archaeological research in the Maya region and currently runs heritage programs with contemporary Maya communities.

Bonnie J. McCay is professor emerita of anthropology at Rutgers University.

Thomas McGovern is a professor with specialization in the fields of environmental and island archaeology and climate change.

John Robert McNeill (b. 1954) is professor of environmental history at Georgetown University. His most famous book is *Something New Under the Sun: An Environmental History of the Twentieth-Century World* (2000).

Montesquieu, Charles–Louis de Secondat, Baron de La Brède et de Montesquieu (1689–1755) was a French lawyer and political philosopher. In *The Spirit of the Laws* he argued that climate might substantially influence the features of man and society.

Dick Peet (b. 1940) is a professor of human geography at Clark University and founder of the journal *Antipode*. He works in politics and ecology.

Benny Peiser (b. 1957) is a social anthropologist at Liverpool John Moores University. He is the director of the Global Warming Policy Foundation.

Plato (c. 424–c.348 B.C.E.) was a philosopher and mathematician, a student of Socrates, and regarded by some as the "father of philosophy."

William Rees (b. 1943) is a professor at the University of British Columbia with research interests in global environmental trends, climate change, and sustainable socioeconomic development.

James Robinson (b. 1960) is an economist and political scientist currently holding a position of professor at the University of Chicago. With Daron Acemoğlu, he wrote *Why Nations Fail: The Origins of*

Power, Prosperity and Poverty (2012). With Jared Diamond, he wrote *Natural Experiments of History* (2010).

Mitt Romney (b. 1947) is an American businessman and Republican politician. He was defeated in the November 2012 presidential election by incumbent Democratic President Barack Obama.

Claire Russell (1919–99) was a psychotherapist, poet, and wife of William M. S. Russell, with whom she worked and published on subjects as diverse as psychoanalysis, animal behavior, and the collapse of ancient civilizations.

William M. S. Russell (1925–2006) was an emeritus professor at Reading University, and the author, with his wife Claire, of *The Myths of Greece and Rome* (2000) and *Population Crisis and Population Cycles* (1999).

Carl Ortwin Sauer (1889–1975) was an American emeritus professor of geography at the University of California at Berkeley. One of his most important contributions to the discipline was his firm criticism of environmental determinism.

Joseph Tainter (b. 1949) is an American anthropologist and historian. He is known for his book *The Collapse of Complex Societies* (1988), which compares the collapse of the Maya, the Chaco, and the Roman Empire.

Rafael Trujillo (1891–1961) was the ruler of the Dominican Republic from 1930 to 1961. His time in power was characterized by top-down violence and repression. However, it brought an era of general stability and economic prosperity.

Andrew P. Vayda (b. 1931) is professor emeritus of anthropology and ecology at Rutgers University and founder of the academic journal *Human Ecology*.

Mike V. Wilcox is associate professor of anthropology at Stanford University. His field of expertise includes the culture and archaeology of the American Southwest. His publications are critical of Diamond's work.

Norman Yoffee (b. 1944) is an Assyriologist (a scholar of the ancient Near Eastern empire of Assyria) and anthropologist who conducted research and published on the Old Babylonian period and the rise and fall of ancient states in comparative perspective.

WORKS CITED

WORKS CITED

Antrosio, Jason. "Jared Diamond and Future Public Anthropology." livinganthropologically.com, July 21, 2014. Accessed September 10, 2015. www.livinganthropologically.com/2014/07/21/jared-diamond-future-public-anthropology/.

"Jared Diamond Won't Beat Mitt Romney – Anthropolitics 2012." livinganthropologically.com, August 4, 2012. Accessed September 10, 2015. www.livinganthropologically.com/2012/08/04/diamond-romney/.

Blaut, James M. "Environmentalism and Eurocentrism." *Geographical Review* 89, no. 3 (1999): 391–408.

Butzer, Karl W. "Cultural Ecology." In *Geography in America*, edited by Gary L. Gaile and Cort J. Willmott, 192–208. Columbus: Merrill, 1989.

Correia, David. "F**k Jared Diamond." *Capitalism Nature Socialism* 24, no. 4 (2013): 1–6.

Crook, Tony. "Indigenous Human Rights." *Anthropology Today* 14, no. 1 (1998): 18–19.

Diamond, Jared M. "About Me." jareddiamond.org, n.d. Accessed September 30, 2015. www.jareddiamond.org/Jared_Diamond/About_Me.html.

Collapse: How Societies Choose to Fail or Survive. London: Penguin, 2011.

"Concentrating Activity of the Gall-bladder." PhD diss. University of Cambridge, 1961.

"Easter's End." *Discover Magazine*, August 1995.

"Geographic Determinism: What Does 'Geographic Determinism' Really Mean?." jareddiamond.org, n.d. Accessed September 30, 2015. www.jareddiamond.org/Jared_Diamond/Geographic_determinism.html.

Guns, Germs, and Steel. London: Random House, 2013.

"The Last Americans: Environmental Collapse and the End of Civilization." *Harper's Magazine*, June 2003.

"Romney Hasn't Done His Homework." *The New York Times,* August 1, 2012. Accessed September 30, 2015. www.nytimes.com/2012/08/02/opinion/mitt-romneys-search-for-simple-answers.html.

"Paradise Lost." *Discover Magazine*, November 1997.

The Third Chimpanzee: The Evolution and Future of the Human Animal. London: HarperCollins, 2006.

"Two Views of Collapse." *Nature* 463, no. 7283 (February 18, 2010): 880–1.

Why Is Sex Fun?: The Evolution Of Human Sexuality. London: Hachette, 2014.

The World Until Yesterday: What Can We Learn from Traditional Societies? New York: Viking, 2013.

Diamond, Jared M., K. David Bishop, and James D. Gilardi. "Geophagy in New Guinea Birds." *Ibis* 141, no. 2 (1999): 181–93.

Diamond, Jared M., and James A. Robinson, eds. *Natural Experiments of History*. Cambridge, MA: Harvard University Press, 2010.

Eriksen, Thomas H. *Engaging Anthropology: The Case for a Public Presence*. Oxford, UK; New York, NY: Berg, 2006.

Esty, Amos. "An Interview with Jared Diamond." *American Scientist Online*, n.d. Accessed September 30, 2015. www.americanscientist.org/bookshelf/pub/jared-diamond.

Fagan, Brian. *Floods, Famines, and Emperors: El Niño and the Fate of Civilizations*. New York: Basic Books, 1999.

Flexner, James L. "Questioning Collapse: Human Resilience, Ecological Vulnerability, and the Aftermath of Empire." *Pacific Affairs* 84, no. 4 (2011): 740–2.

Friedman, Kerim. "From the Archives: Savage Minds vs. Jared Diamond." *Savage Minds*, January 22, 2012. Accessed September 30, 2015. http://savageminds.org/2012/01/22/from-the-archives-savage-minds-vs-jared-diamond/.

Golub, Alex. "Game of Thrones and Anthropology." *Savage Minds*, July 2, 2014. Accessed September 10, 2015. http://savageminds.org/2014/07/02/game-of-thrones-and-anthropology/.

Harris, Marvin. *Cultural Materialism: The Struggle for a Science of Culture*. New York: Random House, 1979.

Hodell, David A., Jason H. Curtis, and Mark Brenner. "Possible Role of Climate in the Collapse of Classic Maya Civilization." *Nature* 375, no. 6530 (1995): 391–4.

Hunt, Terry, and Carl Lipo. "Ecological Catastrophe, Collapse, and the Myth of 'Ecocide' on Rapa Nui (Easter Island)." In *Questioning Collapse: Human Resilience, Ecological Vulnerability, and the Aftermath of Empire*, edited by Patricia A. McAnany and Norman Yoffee, 223–46. New York, NY: Cambridge University Press, 2010.

Ingold, Tim. "Introduction to Culture." In *Companion Encyclopedia of Anthropology*, edited by Tim Ingold, 329–49. London and New York: Routledge, 1994.

Johnson, George. "A Question of Blame When Societies Fall." *The New York Times*, December 25, 2007. Accessed September 30, 2015. www.nytimes. com/2007/12/25/science/25diam.html.

Judkins, Gabriel, Marissa Smith, and Eric Keys. "Determinism within Human–Environment Research and the Rediscovery of Environmental Causation." *The Geographical Journal* 174, no. 1 (2008): 17–29.

Kennedy, Donald. "The Choice: Finding Hope in the History of Environmental Ruin." *Foreign Affairs* 84, no. 2 (2005): 134–8.

Lynas, Mark. "The Myths of Easter Island – Jared Diamond Responds." marklynas.org, September 22, 2011. Accessed September 10, 2015. www. marklynas.org/2011/09/the-myths-of-easter-island-jared-diamond-responds/.

McAnany, Patricia A., and Norman Yoffee, eds. *Questioning Collapse: Human Resilience, Ecological Vulnerability, and the Aftermath of Empire.* New York, NY: Cambridge University Press, 2010.

MacClancy, Jeremy, and Chris McDonaugh, eds. *Popularizing Anthropology.* London: Routledge, 2002.

McGovern, Thomas, Gerald Bigelow, Thomas Amorosi, and Daniel Russell. "Northern Islands, Human Error, and Environmental Degradation: A View of Social and Ecological Change in the Medieval North Atlantic." *Human Ecology* 16, no. 3 (1988): 225–70.

McMichael, Anthony J. "Collapse. How Societies Choose to Fail or Succeed. Jared Diamond." *International Journal of Epidemiology* 35, no. 2 (2006): 499–500.

McMillan, Stephanie. "The Buying and Selling of Jared Diamond." counterpunch.org, December 12, 2009. Accessed September 9, 2015. www. counterpunch.org/2009/12/08/the-buying-and-selling-of-jared-diamond/.

McNeill, John R. "A Usable Past." *American Scientist* 93, no. 2 (2005): 172–5.

Peiser, Benny. "From Genocide to Ecocide: The Rape of Rapa Nui." *Energy & Environment* 16, no. 3 (2005): 513–40.

Penguin Reader's Guide, "A Conversation with Jared Diamond." penguin. com, n.d. Accessed September 9, 2015. www.penguin.com/read/book-clubs/collapse/9780143117001.

Rappaport, Roy A. *Pigs for the Ancestors: Ritual in the Ecology of a New Guinea People.* New Haven: Yale University Press, 1968.

Rees, William. "Contemplating the Abyss." Nature 433, no. 7021 (2005): 15–16.

Russell, Claire, and William M. S. Russell. "Population Crises and Population Cycles." *Medicine, Conflict and Survival* 16, no. 4 (2000): 383–410.

Tainter, Joseph. *The Collapse of Complex Societies.* Cambridge: Cambridge University Press, 1988.

Tett, Gillian. "The Science Interview: Jared Diamond." *Financial Times*, October 11, 2013. Accessed September 30, 2015. www.ft.com/intl/cms/s/2/1f786618-307a-11e3-80a4-00144feab7de.html#axzz3jQUrhdub.

Vayda, Andrew P., and Bonnie J. McCay. "New Directions in Ecology and Ecological Anthropology." *Annual Review of Anthropology* 4 (1975): 293–306.

Wilcox, Michael. "Marketing Conquest and the Vanishing Indian: An Indigenous Response to Jared Diamond's Archaeology of the American Southwest." In *Questioning Collapse: Human Resilience, Ecological Vulnerability, and the Aftermath of Empire*, edited by Patricia A. McAnany and Norman Yoffee, 113–41. New York, NY: Cambridge University Press, 2010.

Williams, Bryn. "Can You Trust Jared Diamond?" *Slate*, February 18, 2013. Accessed September 30, 2015. www.slate.com/articles/health_and_science/books/2013/02/jared_diamond_the_world_until_yesterday_anthropologists_are_wary_of_lack.html.

Yoffee, Norman and George Cowgill, eds. *The Collapse of Ancient States and Civilizations.* Tucson: University of Arizona Press, 1988.

THE MACAT LIBRARY
BY DISCIPLINE

AFRICANA STUDIES

Chinua Achebe's *An Image of Africa: Racism in Conrad's Heart of Darkness*
W. E. B. Du Bois's *The Souls of Black Folk*
Zora Neale Huston's *Characteristics of Negro Expression*
Martin Luther King Jr's *Why We Can't Wait*
Toni Morrison's *Playing in the Dark: Whiteness in the American Literary Imagination*

ANTHROPOLOGY

Arjun Appadurai's *Modernity at Large: Cultural Dimensions of Globalisation*
Philippe Ariès's *Centuries of Childhood*
Franz Boas's *Race, Language and Culture*
Kim Chan & Renée Mauborgne's *Blue Ocean Strategy*
Jared Diamond's *Guns, Germs & Steel: the Fate of Human Societies*
Jared Diamond's *Collapse: How Societies Choose to Fail or Survive*
E. E. Evans-Pritchard's *Witchcraft, Oracles and Magic Among the Azande*
James Ferguson's *The Anti-Politics Machine*
Clifford Geertz's *The Interpretation of Cultures*
David Graeber's *Debt: the First 5000 Years*
Karen Ho's *Liquidated: An Ethnography of Wall Street*
Geert Hofstede's *Culture's Consequences: Comparing Values, Behaviors, Institutes and Organizations across Nations*
Claude Lévi-Strauss's *Structural Anthropology*
Jay Macleod's *Ain't No Makin' It: Aspirations and Attainment in a Low-Income Neighborhood*
Saba Mahmood's *The Politics of Piety: The Islamic Revival and the Feminist Subject*
Marcel Mauss's *The Gift*

BUSINESS

Jean Lave & Etienne Wenger's *Situated Learning*
Theodore Levitt's *Marketing Myopia*
Burton G. Malkiel's *A Random Walk Down Wall Street*
Douglas McGregor's *The Human Side of Enterprise*
Michael Porter's *Competitive Strategy: Creating and Sustaining Superior Performance*
John Kotter's *Leading Change*
C. K. Prahalad & Gary Hamel's *The Core Competence of the Corporation*

CRIMINOLOGY

Michelle Alexander's *The New Jim Crow: Mass Incarceration in the Age of Colorblindness*
Michael R. Gottfredson & Travis Hirschi's *A General Theory of Crime*
Richard Herrnstein & Charles A. Murray's *The Bell Curve: Intelligence and Class Structure in American Life*
Elizabeth Loftus's *Eyewitness Testimony*
Jay Macleod's *Ain't No Makin' It: Aspirations and Attainment in a Low-Income Neighborhood*
Philip Zimbardo's *The Lucifer Effect*

ECONOMICS

Janet Abu-Lughod's *Before European Hegemony*
Ha-Joon Chang's *Kicking Away the Ladder*
David Brion Davis's *The Problem of Slavery in the Age of Revolution*
Milton Friedman's *The Role of Monetary Policy*
Milton Friedman's *Capitalism and Freedom*
David Graeber's *Debt: the First 5000 Years*
Friedrich Hayek's *The Road to Serfdom*
Karen Ho's *Liquidated: An Ethnography of Wall Street*

John Maynard Keynes's *The General Theory of Employment, Interest and Money*
Charles P. Kindleberger's *Manias, Panics and Crashes*
Robert Lucas's *Why Doesn't Capital Flow from Rich to Poor Countries?*
Burton G. Malkiel's *A Random Walk Down Wall Street*
Thomas Robert Malthus's *An Essay on the Principle of Population*
Karl Marx's *Capital*
Thomas Piketty's *Capital in the Twenty-First Century*
Amartya Sen's *Development as Freedom*
Adam Smith's *The Wealth of Nations*
Nassim Nicholas Taleb's *The Black Swan: The Impact of the Highly Improbable*
Amos Tversky's & Daniel Kahneman's *Judgment under Uncertainty: Heuristics and Biases*
Mahbub Ul Haq's *Reflections on Human Development*
Max Weber's *The Protestant Ethic and the Spirit of Capitalism*

FEMINISM AND GENDER STUDIES

Judith Butler's *Gender Trouble*
Simone De Beauvoir's *The Second Sex*
Michel Foucault's *History of Sexuality*
Betty Friedan's *The Feminine Mystique*
Saba Mahmood's *The Politics of Piety: The Islamic Revival and the Feminist Subject*
Joan Wallach Scott's *Gender and the Politics of History*
Mary Wollstonecraft's *A Vindication of the Rights of Woman*
Virginia Woolf's *A Room of One's Own*

GEOGRAPHY

The Brundtland Report's *Our Common Future*
Rachel Carson's *Silent Spring*
Charles Darwin's *On the Origin of Species*
James Ferguson's *The Anti-Politics Machine*
Jane Jacobs's *The Death and Life of Great American Cities*
James Lovelock's *Gaia: A New Look at Life on Earth*
Amartya Sen's *Development as Freedom*
Mathis Wackernagel & William Rees's *Our Ecological Footprint*

HISTORY

Janet Abu-Lughod's *Before European Hegemony*
Benedict Anderson's *Imagined Communities*
Bernard Bailyn's *The Ideological Origins of the American Revolution*
Hanna Batatu's *The Old Social Classes And The Revolutionary Movements Of Iraq*
Christopher Browning's *Ordinary Men: Reserve Police Batallion 101 and the Final Solution in Poland*
Edmund Burke's *Reflections on the Revolution in France*
William Cronon's *Nature's Metropolis: Chicago And The Great West*
Alfred W. Crosby's *The Columbian Exchange*
Hamid Dabashi's *Iran: A People Interrupted*
David Brion Davis's *The Problem of Slavery in the Age of Revolution*
Nathalie Zemon Davis's *The Return of Martin Guerre*
Jared Diamond's *Guns, Germs & Steel: the Fate of Human Societies*
Frank Dikotter's *Mao's Great Famine*
John W Dower's *War Without Mercy: Race And Power In The Pacific War*
W. E. B. Du Bois's *The Souls of Black Folk*
Richard J. Evans's *In Defence of History*
Lucien Febvre's *The Problem of Unbelief in the 16th Century*
Sheila Fitzpatrick's *Everyday Stalinism*

Eric Foner's *Reconstruction: America's Unfinished Revolution, 1863-1877*
Michel Foucault's *Discipline and Punish*
Michel Foucault's *History of Sexuality*
Francis Fukuyama's *The End of History and the Last Man*
John Lewis Gaddis's *We Now Know: Rethinking Cold War History*
Ernest Gellner's *Nations and Nationalism*
Eugene Genovese's *Roll, Jordan, Roll: The World the Slaves Made*
Carlo Ginzburg's *The Night Battles*
Daniel Goldhagen's *Hitler's Willing Executioners*
Jack Goldstone's *Revolution and Rebellion in the Early Modern World*
Antonio Gramsci's *The Prison Notebooks*
Alexander Hamilton, John Jay & James Madison's *The Federalist Papers*
Christopher Hill's *The World Turned Upside Down*
Carole Hillenbrand's *The Crusades: Islamic Perspectives*
Thomas Hobbes's *Leviathan*
Eric Hobsbawm's *The Age Of Revolution*
John A. Hobson's *Imperialism: A Study*
Albert Hourani's *History of the Arab Peoples*
Samuel P. Huntington's *The Clash of Civilizations and the Remaking of World Order*
C. L. R. James's *The Black Jacobins*
Tony Judt's *Postwar: A History of Europe Since 1945*
Ernst Kantorowicz's *The King's Two Bodies: A Study in Medieval Political Theology*
Paul Kennedy's *The Rise and Fall of the Great Powers*
Ian Kershaw's *The "Hitler Myth": Image and Reality in the Third Reich*
John Maynard Keynes's *The General Theory of Employment, Interest and Money*
Charles P. Kindleberger's *Manias, Panics and Crashes*
Martin Luther King Jr's *Why We Can't Wait*
Henry Kissinger's *World Order: Reflections on the Character of Nations and the Course of History*
Thomas Kuhn's *The Structure of Scientific Revolutions*
Georges Lefebvre's *The Coming of the French Revolution*
John Locke's *Two Treatises of Government*
Niccolò Machiavelli's *The Prince*
Thomas Robert Malthus's *An Essay on the Principle of Population*
Mahmood Mamdani's *Citizen and Subject: Contemporary Africa And The Legacy Of Late Colonialism*
Karl Marx's *Capital*
Stanley Milgram's *Obedience to Authority*
John Stuart Mill's *On Liberty*
Thomas Paine's *Common Sense*
Thomas Paine's *Rights of Man*
Geoffrey Parker's *Global Crisis: War, Climate Change and Catastrophe in the Seventeenth Century*
Jonathan Riley-Smith's *The First Crusade and the Idea of Crusading*
Jean-Jacques Rousseau's *The Social Contract*
Joan Wallach Scott's *Gender and the Politics of History*
Theda Skocpol's *States and Social Revolutions*
Adam Smith's *The Wealth of Nations*
Timothy Snyder's *Bloodlands: Europe Between Hitler and Stalin*
Sun Tzu's *The Art of War*
Keith Thomas's *Religion and the Decline of Magic*
Thucydides's *The History of the Peloponnesian War*
Frederick Jackson Turner's *The Significance of the Frontier in American History*
Odd Arne Westad's *The Global Cold War: Third World Interventions And The Making Of Our Times*

LITERATURE

Chinua Achebe's *An Image of Africa: Racism in Conrad's Heart of Darkness*
Roland Barthes's *Mythologies*
Homi K. Bhabha's *The Location of Culture*
Judith Butler's *Gender Trouble*
Simone De Beauvoir's *The Second Sex*
Ferdinand De Saussure's *Course in General Linguistics*
T. S. Eliot's *The Sacred Wood: Essays on Poetry and Criticism*
Zora Neale Huston's *Characteristics of Negro Expression*
Toni Morrison's *Playing in the Dark: Whiteness in the American Literary Imagination*
Edward Said's *Orientalism*
Gayatri Chakravorty Spivak's *Can the Subaltern Speak?*
Mary Wollstonecraft's *A Vindication of the Rights of Women*
Virginia Woolf's *A Room of One's Own*

PHILOSOPHY

Elizabeth Anscombe's *Modern Moral Philosophy*
Hannah Arendt's *The Human Condition*
Aristotle's *Metaphysics*
Aristotle's *Nicomachean Ethics*
Edmund Gettier's *Is Justified True Belief Knowledge?*
Georg Wilhelm Friedrich Hegel's *Phenomenology of Spirit*
David Hume's *Dialogues Concerning Natural Religion*
David Hume's *The Enquiry for Human Understanding*
Immanuel Kant's *Religion within the Boundaries of Mere Reason*
Immanuel Kant's *Critique of Pure Reason*
Søren Kierkegaard's *The Sickness Unto Death*
Søren Kierkegaard's *Fear and Trembling*
C. S. Lewis's *The Abolition of Man*
Alasdair MacIntyre's *After Virtue*
Marcus Aurelius's *Meditations*
Friedrich Nietzsche's *On the Genealogy of Morality*
Friedrich Nietzsche's *Beyond Good and Evil*
Plato's *Republic*
Plato's *Symposium*
Jean-Jacques Rousseau's *The Social Contract*
Gilbert Ryle's *The Concept of Mind*
Baruch Spinoza's *Ethics*
Sun Tzu's *The Art of War*
Ludwig Wittgenstein's *Philosophical Investigations*

POLITICS

Benedict Anderson's *Imagined Communities*
Aristotle's *Politics*
Bernard Bailyn's *The Ideological Origins of the American Revolution*
Edmund Burke's *Reflections on the Revolution in France*
John C. Calhoun's *A Disquisition on Government*
Ha-Joon Chang's *Kicking Away the Ladder*
Hamid Dabashi's *Iran: A People Interrupted*
Hamid Dabashi's *Theology of Discontent: The Ideological Foundation of the Islamic Revolution in Iran*
Robert Dahl's *Democracy and its Critics*
Robert Dahl's *Who Governs?*
David Brion Davis's *The Problem of Slavery in the Age of Revolution*

Alexis De Tocqueville's *Democracy in America*
James Ferguson's *The Anti-Politics Machine*
Frank Dikotter's *Mao's Great Famine*
Sheila Fitzpatrick's *Everyday Stalinism*
Eric Foner's *Reconstruction: America's Unfinished Revolution, 1863-1877*
Milton Friedman's *Capitalism and Freedom*
Francis Fukuyama's *The End of History and the Last Man*
John Lewis Gaddis's *We Now Know: Rethinking Cold War History*
Ernest Gellner's *Nations and Nationalism*
David Graeber's *Debt: the First 5000 Years*
Antonio Gramsci's *The Prison Notebooks*
Alexander Hamilton, John Jay & James Madison's *The Federalist Papers*
Friedrich Hayek's *The Road to Serfdom*
Christopher Hill's *The World Turned Upside Down*
Thomas Hobbes's *Leviathan*
John A. Hobson's *Imperialism: A Study*
Samuel P. Huntington's *The Clash of Civilizations and the Remaking of World Order*
Tony Judt's *Postwar: A History of Europe Since 1945*
David C. Kang's *China Rising: Peace, Power and Order in East Asia*
Paul Kennedy's *The Rise and Fall of Great Powers*
Robert Keohane's *After Hegemony*
Martin Luther King Jr.'s *Why We Can't Wait*
Henry Kissinger's *World Order: Reflections on the Character of Nations and the Course of History*
John Locke's *Two Treatises of Government*
Niccolò Machiavelli's *The Prince*
Thomas Robert Malthus's *An Essay on the Principle of Population*
Mahmood Mamdani's *Citizen and Subject: Contemporary Africa And The Legacy Of Late Colonialism*
Karl Marx's *Capital*
John Stuart Mill's *On Liberty*
John Stuart Mill's *Utilitarianism*
Hans Morgenthau's *Politics Among Nations*
Thomas Paine's *Common Sense*
Thomas Paine's *Rights of Man*
Thomas Piketty's *Capital in the Twenty-First Century*
Robert D. Putman's *Bowling Alone*
John Rawls's *Theory of Justice*
Jean-Jacques Rousseau's *The Social Contract*
Theda Skocpol's *States and Social Revolutions*
Adam Smith's *The Wealth of Nations*
Sun Tzu's *The Art of War*
Henry David Thoreau's *Civil Disobedience*
Thucydides's *The History of the Peloponnesian War*
Kenneth Waltz's *Theory of International Politics*
Max Weber's *Politics as a Vocation*
Odd Arne Westad's *The Global Cold War: Third World Interventions And The Making Of Our Times*

POSTCOLONIAL STUDIES

Roland Barthes's *Mythologies*
Frantz Fanon's *Black Skin, White Masks*
Homi K. Bhabha's *The Location of Culture*
Gustavo Gutiérrez's *A Theology of Liberation*
Edward Said's *Orientalism*
Gayatri Chakravorty Spivak's *Can the Subaltern Speak?*

PSYCHOLOGY

Gordon Allport's *The Nature of Prejudice*
Alan Baddeley & Graham Hitch's *Aggression: A Social Learning Analysis*
Albert Bandura's *Aggression: A Social Learning Analysis*
Leon Festinger's *A Theory of Cognitive Dissonance*
Sigmund Freud's *The Interpretation of Dreams*
Betty Friedan's *The Feminine Mystique*
Michael R. Gottfredson & Travis Hirschi's *A General Theory of Crime*
Eric Hoffer's *The True Believer: Thoughts on the Nature of Mass Movements*
William James's *Principles of Psychology*
Elizabeth Loftus's *Eyewitness Testimony*
A. H. Maslow's *A Theory of Human Motivation*
Stanley Milgram's *Obedience to Authority*
Steven Pinker's *The Better Angels of Our Nature*
Oliver Sacks's *The Man Who Mistook His Wife For a Hat*
Richard Thaler & Cass Sunstein's *Nudge: Improving Decisions About Health, Wealth and Happiness*
Amos Tversky's *Judgment under Uncertainty: Heuristics and Biases*
Philip Zimbardo's *The Lucifer Effect*

SCIENCE

Rachel Carson's *Silent Spring*
William Cronon's *Nature's Metropolis: Chicago And The Great West*
Alfred W. Crosby's *The Columbian Exchange*
Charles Darwin's *On the Origin of Species*
Richard Dawkin's *The Selfish Gene*
Thomas Kuhn's *The Structure of Scientific Revolutions*
Geoffrey Parker's *Global Crisis: War, Climate Change and Catastrophe in the Seventeenth Century*
Mathis Wackernagel & William Rees's *Our Ecological Footprint*

SOCIOLOGY

Michelle Alexander's *The New Jim Crow: Mass Incarceration in the Age of Colorblindness*
Gordon Allport's *The Nature of Prejudice*
Albert Bandura's *Aggression: A Social Learning Analysis*
Hanna Batatu's *The Old Social Classes And The Revolutionary Movements Of Iraq*
Ha-Joon Chang's *Kicking Away the Ladder*
W. E. B. Du Bois's *The Souls of Black Folk*
Émile Durkheim's *On Suicide*
Frantz Fanon's *Black Skin, White Masks*
Frantz Fanon's *The Wretched of the Earth*
Eric Foner's *Reconstruction: America's Unfinished Revolution, 1863-1877*
Eugene Genovese's *Roll, Jordan, Roll: The World the Slaves Made*
Jack Goldstone's *Revolution and Rebellion in the Early Modern World*
Antonio Gramsci's *The Prison Notebooks*
Richard Herrnstein & Charles A Murray's *The Bell Curve: Intelligence and Class Structure in American Life*
Eric Hoffer's *The True Believer: Thoughts on the Nature of Mass Movements*
Jane Jacobs's *The Death and Life of Great American Cities*
Robert Lucas's *Why Doesn't Capital Flow from Rich to Poor Countries?*
Jay Macleod's *Ain't No Makin' It: Aspirations and Attainment in a Low Income Neighborhood*
Elaine May's *Homeward Bound: American Families in the Cold War Era*
Douglas McGregor's *The Human Side of Enterprise*
C. Wright Mills's *The Sociological Imagination*

Thomas Piketty's *Capital in the Twenty-First Century*
Robert D. Putman's *Bowling Alone*
David Riesman's *The Lonely Crowd: A Study of the Changing American Character*
Edward Said's *Orientalism*
Joan Wallach Scott's *Gender and the Politics of History*
Theda Skocpol's *States and Social Revolutions*
Max Weber's *The Protestant Ethic and the Spirit of Capitalism*

THEOLOGY

Augustine's *Confessions*
Benedict's *Rule of St Benedict*
Gustavo Gutiérrez's *A Theology of Liberation*
Carole Hillenbrand's *The Crusades: Islamic Perspectives*
David Hume's *Dialogues Concerning Natural Religion*
Immanuel Kant's *Religion within the Boundaries of Mere Reason*
Ernst Kantorowicz's *The King's Two Bodies: A Study in Medieval Political Theology*
Søren Kierkegaard's *The Sickness Unto Death*
C. S. Lewis's *The Abolition of Man*
Saba Mahmood's *The Politics of Piety: The Islamic Revival and the Feminist Subject*
Baruch Spinoza's *Ethics*
Keith Thomas's *Religion and the Decline of Magic*

COMING SOON

Chris Argyris's *The Individual and the Organisation*
Seyla Benhabib's *The Rights of Others*
Walter Benjamin's *The Work Of Art in the Age of Mechanical Reproduction*
John Berger's *Ways of Seeing*
Pierre Bourdieu's *Outline of a Theory of Practice*
Mary Douglas's *Purity and Danger*
Roland Dworkin's *Taking Rights Seriously*
James G. March's *Exploration and Exploitation in Organisational Learning*
Ikujiro Nonaka's *A Dynamic Theory of Organizational Knowledge Creation*
Griselda Pollock's *Vision and Difference*
Amartya Sen's *Inequality Re-Examined*
Susan Sontag's *On Photography*
Yasser Tabbaa's *The Transformation of Islamic Art*
Ludwig von Mises's *Theory of Money and Credit*

Macat Disciplines

Access the greatest ideas and thinkers across entire disciplines, including

Postcolonial Studies

Roland Barthes's *Mythologies*
Frantz Fanon's *Black Skin, White Masks*
Homi K. Bhabha's *The Location of Culture*
Gustavo Gutiérrez's *A Theology of Liberation*
Edward Said's *Orientalism*
Gayatri Chakravorty Spivak's *Can the Subaltern Speak?*

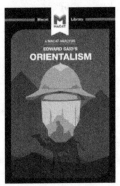

Macat analyses are available from all good bookshops and libraries.

Access hundreds of analyses through one, multimedia tool.
Join free for one month **library.macat.com**

Macat Pairs

Analyse historical and modern issues from opposite sides of an argument. Pairs include:

HOW TO RUN AN ECONOMY

John Maynard Keynes's
The General Theory OF Employment, Interest and Money

Classical economics suggests that market economies are self-correcting in times of recession or depression, and tend toward full employment and output. But English economist John Maynard Keynes disagrees.

In his ground-breaking 1936 study *The General Theory*, Keynes argues that traditional economics has misunderstood the causes of unemployment. Employment is not determined by the price of labor; it is directly linked to demand. Keynes believes market economies are by nature unstable, and so require government intervention. Spurred on by the social catastrophe of the Great Depression of the 1930s, he sets out to revolutionize the way the world thinks

Milton Friedman's
The Role of Monetary Policy

Friedman's 1968 paper changed the course of economic theory. In just 17 pages, he demolished existing theory and outlined an effective alternate monetary policy designed to secure 'high employment, stable prices and rapid growth.'

Friedman demonstrated that monetary policy plays a vital role in broader economic stability and argued that economists got their monetary policy wrong in the 1950s and 1960s by misunderstanding the relationship between inflation and unemployment. Previous generations of economists had believed that governments could permanently decrease unemployment by permitting inflation—and vice versa. Friedman's most original contribution was to show that this supposed trade-off is an illusion that only works in the short term.

Macat analyses are available from all good bookshops and libraries.

Access hundreds of analyses through one, multimedia tool.
Join free for one month **library.macat.com**

Macat Disciplines

Access the greatest ideas and thinkers across entire disciplines, including

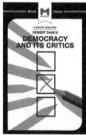   

Printed in the United States
by Baker & Taylor Publisher Services